To Erika,

You are fabulous!

I enjoyed working with you at Skyline so much. You are a true Young Southern Lady. Your 'mama' would be proud of what a great job you do!

Sharon

2014

Sharon McGukin

Flowers of the heart

a bride's guide
to choosing flowers
for her wedding

Wedding designs brides love!

Sharon McGukin

Principal Photographer - Douglas McGukin

Contributing Photographers
Jim Celuch
Diane Douglass
Allison Dudley
Karen Goforth
Glenn Holmes
Jennifer Kemp
Jim Maguire
Eric McCarty
TimMcClain
Ron Parks
Rob Roux
Ron White

Floral Trend Publications

Floral Designs & Art Direction by
Sharon McGukin

Principal Photographer
Douglas McGukin

Contributing Photographers
Jim Celuch
Diane Douglass
Allison Dudley
Karen Goforth
Glenn Holmes
Jennifer Kemp
Jim Maguire
Eric McCarty
Tim McClain
Ron Parks
Rob Roux
Ron White

Graphic Layout
Dana Wedman

Copy Editor
Cathleen Martinez

First Published in USA, 2009
Floral Trend Publications
915 Dixie Street
Carrollton, GA 30117 USA

ISBN 10 - 0615292224
ISBN 13 - 978-0-615-29222-9
Printed in USA

This book can be ordered by mail:
Floral Trend Publications
915 Dixie Street
Carrollton, GA 30117 USA

Online:
www.sharonmcgukin.com

To my husband Tim, whose constant words of encouragement & bouquets of flowers sustain me. Thank you for the years of love & laughter.

And to our children Drew, Shea & Kane, thank you for the joy you bring to us. We've learned many lessons of life seeing it through your eyes.

Introduction

"All the details that go astray will create the stories of your wedding day that make it all your own."

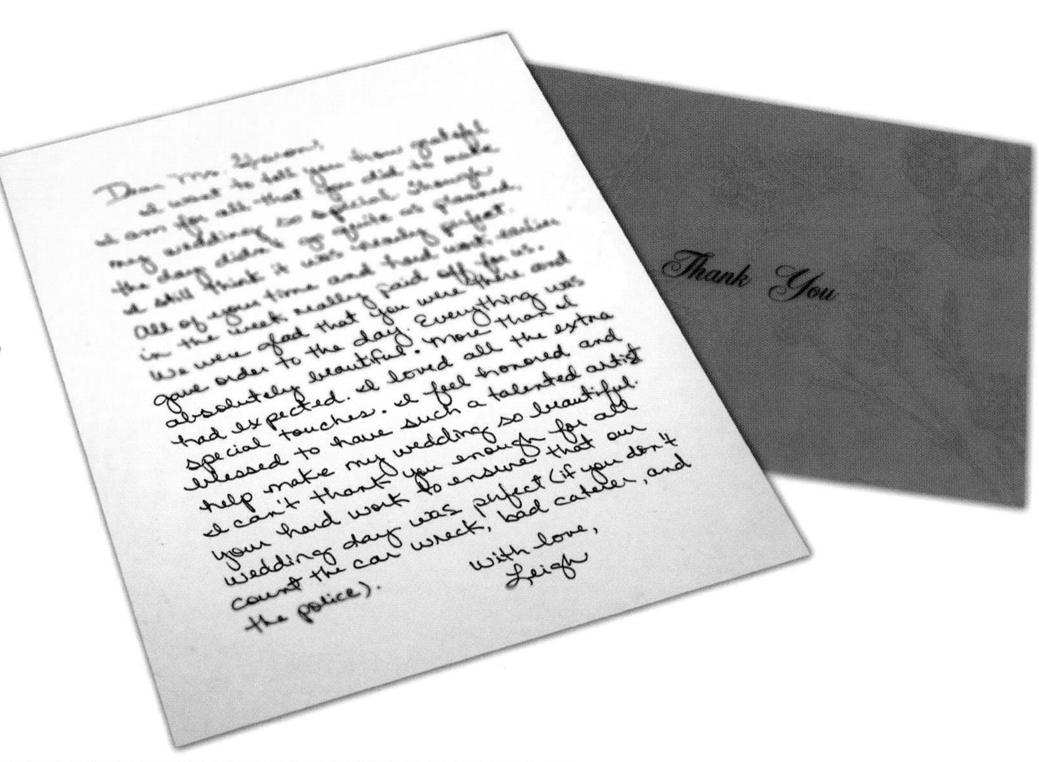

Dear Mrs. [illegible],
I want to tell you how grateful
I am for all that you did to make
my wedding so special. Though
the day didn't go quite as planned,
I still think it was really perfect.
All of your time and hard work earlier
in the week really paid off for us.
We were glad that you were there and
gave order to the day. Everything was
absolutely beautiful. More than I
had expected. I loved all the extra
special touches. I feel honored and
blessed to have such a talented artist
help make my wedding so beautiful.
I can't thank you enough for all
your hard work to ensure that our
wedding day was perfect (if you don't
count the car wreck, bad caterer, and
the police).
With love,
Leigh

Wedding Memories

You're engaged! Congratulations. This is an exciting time for you and your fiancé. You have so much to do and so many plans to make, but some day you will look back at these hectic days with a feeling of special fondness for the wedding memories that you are now creating.

I fell in love with weddings when designing flowers for my own ceremony in 1975. Typical of a young 70's bride, I carried a huge bouquet of daisies and roses accented by strands of ribbons and pearls. Our photos show lots of lace for the bride, ruffles on the men's tux shirts, orchids pinned on moms, pink summer hats for the bridesmaids, and don't forget the platform shoes worn by all. We thought it was perfect.

Once the 70's hippie inspired fashions had passed, it took many years for me to be able to look back at my wedding photos without regret. The bouquet I had created was too large for me. The bridesmaid dresses much too pink and ruffled in their then popular dotted Swiss look. Years later I discussed weddings with a new friend who had married in another part of the state during our same year. She shared her photos with me and to my surprise and relief her photos looked almost identical to mine. Those overdone looks had been the style, not just a lapse in good judgment on my part. I have always loved the newest trends, a fact that is sadly evident in our wedding photos.

Over thirty years later, I am still happily married to my high school sweetheart and continue to love designing flowers for weddings. I enjoy sharing the excitement of the new couple by directing their families and wedding attendants through the events of the day. However, I now encourage brides to use current trends cautiously, warning that they can become dated in the photos, as did mine.

A wedding is a celebration of the heart. It is a special time when two families come together to become one extended family. It should include the treasured religious, cultural, and traditional celebrations of each, along with beautiful flowers to commemorate the event. The joy is in sharing the moment surrounded by loved ones, who join you in celebration. Relax. Enjoy. Share your joy by taking into consideration the feelings and comfort of your guests as you plan the wedding events. Yes, it is your wedding, but if you are a loving and gracious bride the day is not just 'all about you'! Try to create an intimate time of happiness for all.

Plan perfectly in advance, yet know your wedding will not be perfect. Nothing in life really is. That's okay. This is a real life celebration, a dress rehearsal for all the mishaps of sharing your life together, not a pageant to be performed with perfection. All the details that go astray will create the stories of your wedding day that make it all your own. No matter how large or small the event, how perfect or imperfect the detail, relax and allow yourself to fall in love with your own wedding memories.

Sharon McGukin

Table of contents

Spring

Summer

Autumn

Winter

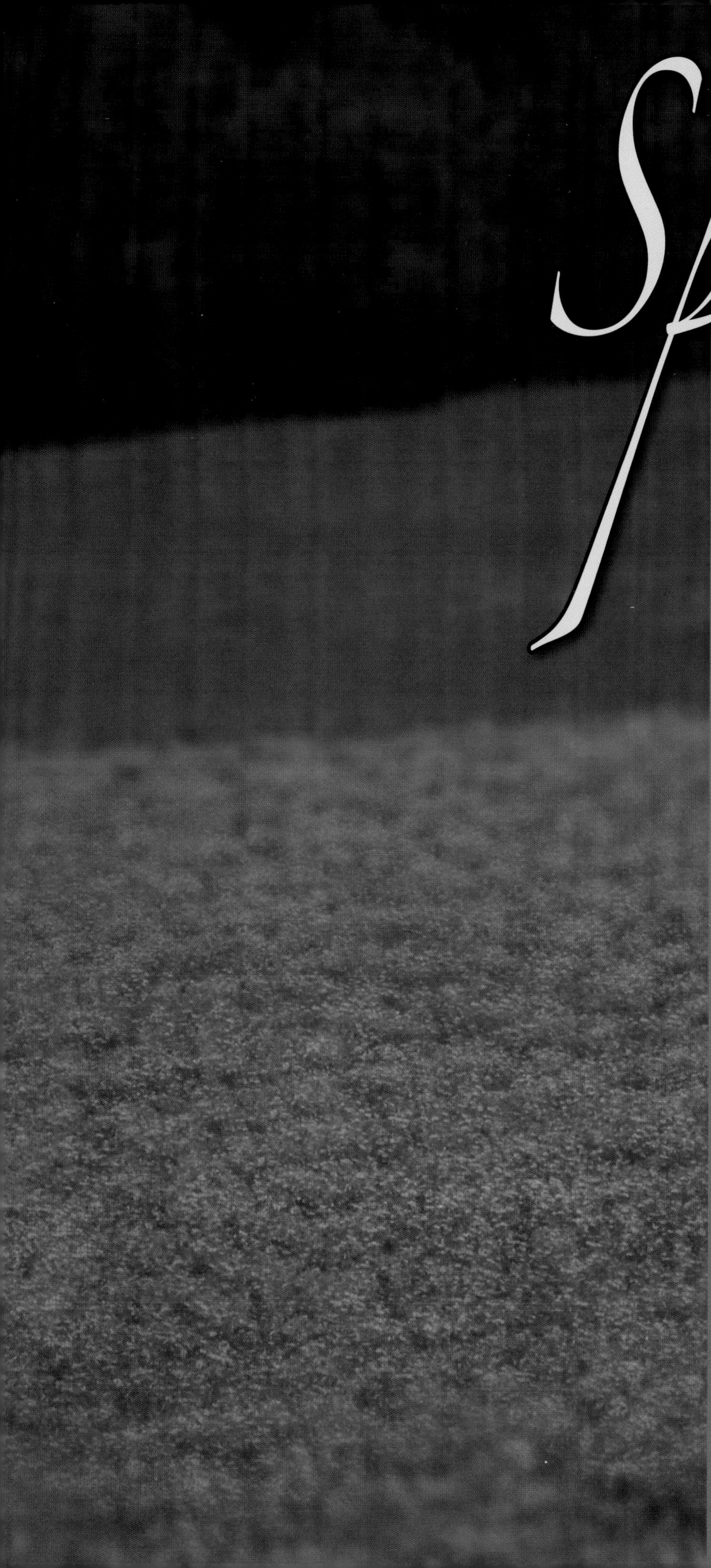

Spring

A
time
of
new
beginnings

Creating your floral plan

If you are like most brides, you know that flowers are important and have added them to your list of things to consider early in your planning stages. However, when it comes to actually creating a floral plan, you may be wondering where you should begin.

Selecting your florist

First, shop for the perfect wedding gown, one that makes you feel like a princess. Then, select pretty bridesmaid dresses that are flattering to your attendants and compliment your gown. Having accomplished those tasks, you know it is important to accessorize both with beautiful flowers that enhance your day and look great in wedding photos. Don't know a lot about fresh flowers? Begin by surfing the web and printing out images of pretty bouquets, tearing out magazine pages of flowers in your favorite colors, and asking friends and family if you can look at their wedding photos for ideas. At this time, you may want to consider hiring a professional florist to advise you in combining all the ideas you have collected into a coherent plan. It is important to find a floral designer who you will enjoy working with as you plan the floral décor for your wedding.

Start early

It is wise to start your search early. Many brides begin as soon as they set the date and secure their facility - as early as nine to twelve months in advance. Competent professional florists, who are creative and efficient, are often very much in demand and are booked far in advance. The earlier you begin the process the more likely the designer of your choice will have the space in their schedule for your event. If you don't have a favorite florist, ask friends and relatives for referrals. Ask the other wedding professionals you have hired such as the bridal shop, caterer, or photographer for recommendations of local florists they prefer to work with. Visit the web sites and design studios of designers that you are considering and ask to see photos or videos of their work. If their design work is unknown to you, ask them to provide a list of names of recent brides you can contact for a referral. If you still can't decide on a specific florist, narrow your list of potential candidates to two or three floral designers whose design style you prefer and make appointments with them for consultation.

Roses
Lily Grass
Hypericum
French Tulips
Cymbidium Orchids
Pearls Strung onto Bear Grass

D

Develop a budget

One of the most difficult parts of planning a wedding is to realistically look at the costs involved. The calculation of what will be spent on a wedding is often determined by family dynamics. Traditionally, the bride's parents pay for most of the wedding costs including the ceremony, bride's portion of the flower list, and the cost of hosting the reception. The groom's family typically contributes by covering the expense of the rehearsal dinner, the groom's list of flowers, and perhaps a groom's cake. Today many couples are waiting until they are older and established in their careers to marry, so they choose to pay for a large portion of their wedding themselves. This allows them to plan their wedding as they wish. Sometimes one family is more financially capable of paying for the wedding and they choose to do so. In the case of divorced families, perhaps one parent is more capable of contributing financially while another has more time or a special talent such as sewing, baking or designing. Whatever works for the couple and the two families is perfectly acceptable. The most important factor is to sit down with all parties and make an open agreement on how much will be spent and how the division of money, time, or effort will be assigned to each family member so all feel included and appreciated.

Characteristics to look for in a professional florist:

- Recognizable style of work
- Offers referrals from previous brides
- Punctual, attentive to detail
- Well-organized during the consultation
- Willing to work within your budget
- Offers creative ideas, but hears your suggestions
- Doesn't over book their staff
- Works well with other local vendors
- Provides photos of their work
- Knowledgeable of price and selection by season

Características que debe buscar en un florista profesional:

- Reconocible estilo de trabajo
- Ofrece referencias de los anteriores novias
- Puntual, atento a los detalles
- Bien organizados en la consulta
- Dispuestos a trabajar dentro de su presupuesto
- Ofrece ideas creativas, sino que escucha sus sugerencias
- No más de libro de las capacidades de su personal
- Funciona bien con otros proveedores locales
- Ofrece fotos de su trabajo como ejemplos
- Conocimientos y la selección de los precios por temporada

Roses
Reindeer Moss
Seeded Eucalyptus Buds
Foam Based Bouquet Holder
Smithers-Oasis® Silver Aluminum Wire
Pearls Strung on Silver Bouillon
Smithers-Oasis® 8 Inch Silver Wire Collar

Balance is key

When planning your budget, remember that your flowers must be in balance with all other elements of the wedding for a cohesive look. An investment in elegant facilities, exquisite dresses, large guest list, and bountiful food displays can be diminished visually if you skimp on finishing details such as the flowers. Brides who aren't careful of their budget in the beginning when buying dresses and securing locations can run out of money at the end when it is time to select these most noticeable details. Flowers are often the first thing noticed by guests, and a highlight of the wedding photos. Keep in mind that a large wedding has the need for abundant flower displays, while a small, simple ceremony in a well landscaped garden may need much less. Utilize the beauty and fragrance of flowers to an advantage on your wedding day.

Look at the total amount of money you can afford to invest in your wedding. Before making any purchases, break down the costs by categories such as facility, food, alcohol, attire, photography, flowers, rental, invitations, guest favors, etc. Try to estimate the price range for each category. Set a price range for each category that will keep the look of the wedding in balance. For example, don't spend so much money on flowers that you must skimp and not have a wedding cake. In that same spirit, don't spend so much on food and alcohol that the flowers look like an afterthought. You will be less stressed and your guests will be more impressed if you plan from the beginning to keep every area of the wedding in balance.

Do your homework

To prepare for a productive consultation, do your homework in advance. Create an outline of the basic information regarding your wedding details. Confirm the date, time, and location of your wedding and create a list of that information. Include a list of the names and contact information of wedding professionals such as the bridal consultant, caterer, photographer, etc. that you have already secured. Tally the number of people in your wedding party and list the number of personal flowers that will be required for them. Request a list of rules and regulations from the ceremony facility that will apply to your florist and make a copy for their files. If you think the florist might be unfamiliar with the facility, provide photos or layout sketches of the areas to be used. Estimate the number of guests and number of guest tables, etc. Develop a list of flowers needed for areas such as the altar, pews, buffet tables, guest tables, etc. Jot down any religious or family traditions involving flowers that you might like to include. Prepare a list of any additional questions that you might have for the florist.

Flower-Savvy Tip:

Appeal to the five senses of the guests when planning your wedding decorations in order to surround them with a memorable experience. Sight – interesting floral displays, Smell – fragrant flowers and foods, Touch - textural materials, Taste – delightful flavors, Hearing – musical inspiration.

Roses
Dendrobium Orchids
Camellia Leaves
Foam Based Bouquet Holder

Order your dresses first

Prior to setting up a consultation with the florist, be sure to have purchased or ordered your bridesmaids dresses. Take to the meeting a swatch of the bridesmaids' dress fabric to help determine floral color harmony. The color, style, and formality of the dress will determine the color and variety of flowers that can be chosen. The type of flower and number of stems used in a design determines the price of the bouquet. Dye lots can vary, specific styles can be unavailable for your timetable, dresses can be backordered, and perhaps a change in dresses would require a change in flowers. To keep from wasting your valuable time and your florist's, be sure that the dresses have been ordered and you are given an approximate delivery date prior to spending time in consultation ordering flowers.

Selecting a florist

- Organize the date, time, and location
- Set a budget for wedding costs
- Order bride and bridesmaids dresses
- Gather photos of flower designs
- Visit websites and design studios
- Set up a consultation appointment
- Get an outline of flowers and cost
- Pay a deposit to secure the day
- Assign "deal with it days" for follow-up
- Establish date for final payment

Selección de un florista

- Organizar la fecha, hora y lugar
- Establezca un presupuesto para gastos de boda
- Ordenar los vestidos de la novia y las damas de honor
- Reunir fotos de los diseños de flores
- Visite los sitios web y estudios de diseño floral
- Separar fecha de orientación con el florista
- Obtener un resumen de las flores y el costo
- Pagar un depósito para garantizar el la fecha de evento

Flower-Savvy Tip:

Develop a list of names and cell phone numbers of wedding participants and vendors to make instant communication possible in case of unexpected questions or emergencies. Along with the wedding couple and their parents, copies should be provided to your florist, wedding director, caterer, photographer, facility contact, and wedding party.

You can create the look of a faux garden rose by taking a wide open rose and pulling the very center petals out to leave the center exposed.

Roses
Dendrobium Orchid Blooms
Seeded Eucalyptus Buds
Smithers-Oasis® 8 Inch Gold Wire Collar

S

Set up appointments

Call in advance to set up an appointment for the purpose of discussing your wedding flowers. Ask if it is possible to discuss your plans with the person who will actually create your designs on your wedding day. Ask how many weddings will be scheduled on the same day as yours. If the shop indicates that they typically schedule heavily, ask if they ever have difficulty staffing that many events. Above all, seek a designer who is willing to invest their time and energy in helping your wedding day run smoothly. Look for an individual who is interested in both hearing your ideas and sharing their own suggestions. Ask to see photos of their designs and show photos that you have collected of your favorite styles. Ask them to work with you within your budget, or if you don't have an established budget ask them to give you three prices such as budget, average, and exceptional for each design category so that you can decide which is best for your overall plan. After you have made your selections for the entire wedding, ask for an overall estimate. A good designer can work within your budget and can estimate a price range of projected costs by totaling the selections you have made thus far and suggesting areas that are frequently expanded. Ask the florist what changes or additions they might suggest if you find that you have additional funds to invest in flowers once you have finalized plans for the other areas of expense. If you find that you are over budget with your choices, ask the florist to assist you in making cuts, as they know where the changes will be less noticeable.

Seek someone you connect with

It is important to select as your wedding florist someone who is knowledgeable of their product, gives you a clear idea of projected cost, makes you feel comfortable working with them and makes you feel confident in their ability to deliver on their promises. Look for someone who listens carefully and offers professional advice based on your ideas. Be sure that they are accurately listing all details during the consultation.

Cymbidium Orchids
Miniature Callas
Plumosa
Stephanotis
Pearl Beaded Garland

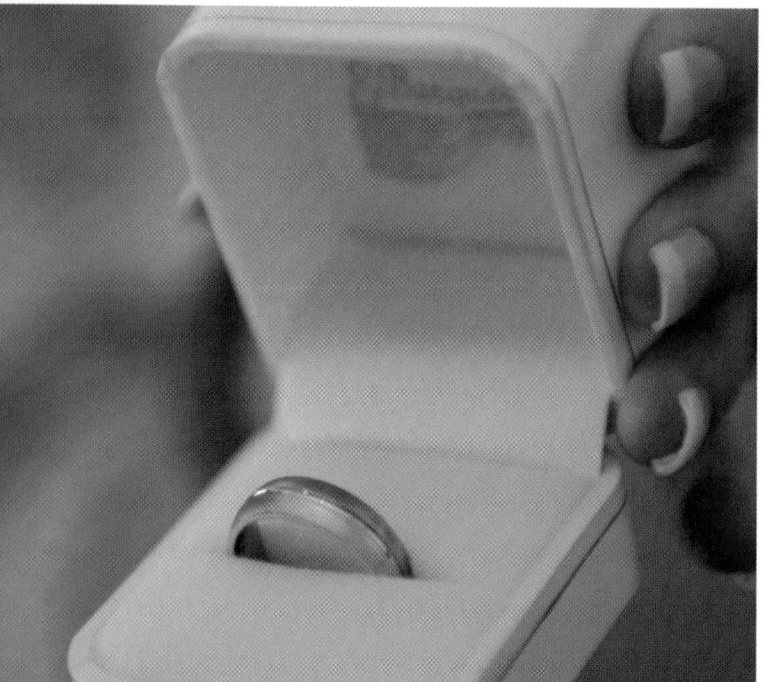

Pre-consultation preparation for Brides:

- Collect photos of designs, styles, colors that you like and dislike
- Create a list of wedding participants for accurate numbers
- Provide a color swatch of the dress fabrics (dresses must be ordered)
- Bring any contracts or lists of rules and regulations for facilities
- If the florist hasn't worked in your facility, meet there or provide photos
- Develop list of special needs, i.e. handicapped family members, small children, etc.
- Provide swatches of any linens or fabrics to be used in decor
- Outline a basic floral budget

La preparación para la pre-consulta con Novias:

- Reunir fotos de diseños, los estilos, los colores que usted quiere
- Crea una lista de Asistentes
- Proporciona una muestra de color de la tela de los vestidos
- Trae contrato de la facilidades con la listas de reglas y regulaciones
- Si el florista no ha trabajado en el lugar de la actividad, reunete en el lugar
- Desarrolla una lista de necesidades especiales.
- Proporciona muestras de cualquier tela o tejidos para ser utilizadas.
- Provee un presupuesto básico para los arreglos florales

Flower-Savvy Tip:

To open lily blooms more quickly, strip all leaves from the lily stem except for one or two at the top. Cut the stems closer to the length you will be using them with the diagonal cut of a sharp knife. Place in 5″ to 7″ of warm water. Remove lily stamens from opened blooms and drop them into the water. This will cause a chemical reaction that makes the closed blooms open faster. If the blooms are really tight you can also speed up the process by placing plastic bags over the flower heads and top of the bucket and placing it in a warm area. You can also place the bucket in an area of indirect, bright, warm sunlight to encourage blooms to open.

Ivy
Sprengeri
Oriental Lilies
Foam Based Bouquet Holder

Rental items

In advance, list items you will need to rent such as tent, tables, chairs, linens, vases, candelabra, trellis, potted plants, etc. Ask if the florist rents these items or ask for a referral of a rental company that they have had success in working with. Once you have your event layout diagram, make a list of the names and numbers of items needed, contact a local rental company to set up an appointment to outline your needs and get an estimate of cost. Ask for a guarantee of delivery and removal times.

On-site installation

After having selected flowers and developed a budget, it is time to discuss installation and removal of flowers. Provide the florist with rules and regulations of installation and delivery policies from your facility. Ask if the florist will provide installation of the flowers. If so, ask for a timeline and an estimate of costs for on-site labor and delivery. Ask how long it will take them to set up the decorations and make sure everything is in order. Request that they guarantee a completion time well in advance of the photographer's arrival. Ask specific questions regarding the difference in cost if you pick up your flowers vs. having them delivered. If flowers are simply to be dropped off, what is the delivery fee? If you choose this option you will need to assign someone to be on site to receive the delivery, place the floral arrangements, and pin on personal flowers.

Determine what will be involved with the task of dismantling the event. Who will be responsible for the removal of flowers? Where will the materials go? What costs are involved? If you are on a tight budget and planning a very simple service this is an area where you could cut costs by enlisting close friends or family to assist by picking up the flowers from the florist, cleaning up, and disposing of the flowers after the ceremony. For a larger event you will want to hire professionals for both the installation and removal of your flowers.

Flower-Savvy Tip:

Strategically placing an abundance of gardenias or other such fragrant flowers throughout the decorated areas heightens the sense of smell for guests and makes them more cognizant of the flowers used for decoration. Before using this technique be sure that no one in the wedding party is overly allergic to the fragrance of flowers.

Gladiolus
Oriental Lily
Rose
Curly Willow
Plumosa

Formality and style

Use flowers to express formality and style
The beauty and color harmony of your flowers can be used to continue a theme, indicate a style, or reflect the formality of your wedding events. Colorful flowers of interesting shapes may seem visually less formal. Using bold-colored flowers of energetic shapes such as gerbera daisies or tropical favorites like anthurium and bird of paradise can add a festive flair. To create an exotic look, use minimalist designs of branches, lilies, and orchids of intense color and textural interest. To achieve a more formal look, utilize the simplistic elegance of mono-botanical or monochromatic arrangements using one type of flower or color. Delicate flowers such as roses, hydrangea and callas are popular choices for creating formal linear or round bouquets. After setting the date of your wedding, securing the facilities with a deposit, and determining the style and formality of the event, it is time to establish the color harmony of your wedding.

Peonies
Lilacs
#40 Double French Satin Ribbon

Choosing a color harmony for the wedding

Deciding on a color harmony for your wedding is one of the first major decisions regarding the floral décor. The color of dresses, environment, and flowers must be in visual harmony for the photographs to reflect a unified look. One method is to begin by choosing from your personal favorite colors. Most people have a preference for either deep, rich colors or soft, muted ones; decide which level of color intensity best suits your personal taste. Next consider the colors that might look most flattering on your attendants. The combination of their skin and hair tones should be taken into consideration when choosing bridesmaid gowns. Remember to include the color of your bridal gown in potential color palettes as you will be photographed together often. Visit the wedding facility to look at the interior colors such as carpeting, drapes, upholstery fabrics, etc. Be sure your choice of wedding color palette coordinates with this setting for a harmonious look.

Having a basic color range in mind, begin to shop for the style of bridesmaid dress that you prefer. Then, check to see if your selection is available in a color that fits within your chosen palette. After purchasing or placing an order for the bridal gown and bridesmaids dresses it is time to hire a florist. A knowledgeable florist can offer professional advice about the varieties of flowers available in your season and which colors, shapes, and textures will compliment your dresses.

Dividing the expense of the flower list

Traditional division of who pays for what flowers varies by region, religion, and local custom. Your florist can best help you decide how the floral expenses are typically divided in your area. A traditional rule of thumb is that the bride's family is responsible for the groom's boutonniere, the personal flowers for the bridesmaids, flowers girls, cake servers, musicians, readers, and any other honored guests. They are also responsible for the flowers and rentals for the wedding ceremony and reception. If they choose to place flowers at the hotel for guests, the expense will be added to their list. The same applies if thank-you flowers are sent to individuals who were especially helpful throughout the wedding season. As for the groom's family, they traditionally pay for the bride, mothers, grandmothers, and groomsmen, ushers, ring bearers, fathers, grandfathers, and clergy. Often flowers used at the rehearsal dinner by the groom's family can be incorporated with the reception flowers the next day. If this is the plan, it is a good idea to coordinate the flowers through the same florist. Ask if there is a relocation fee for picking up the flowers from the rehearsal venue and delivering them to the reception site. Sometimes one person, or family, is more passionate about flowers than others and will offer to cover the cost of all the flowers in order to have the option of deciding the volume, style, and expense of those used. If the flowers for various segments of the wedding are to be designed by different people, be sure to outline a theme, flower selection, and color harmony for all, so there is visual harmony throughout the events. If the bride and groom choose to send flowers to their parents after the wedding it is at their expense.

Flower-Savvy Tip:

If flowers such as stems of orchids, callas, hydrangea, roses, or lilies are fresh but dehydrated, submerge the entire stem into lukewarm water and allow them to stay submerged until the water cools. Then, remove the stems, give each a sharp diagonal cut, and place in a reservoir of fresh warm water with flower food.

Roses
Hydrangeas

Securing your florist

Pay a deposit
When you feel comfortable that you have selected a floral designer that you can enjoy working with, pay a deposit to hold their services for the day of your wedding. Request a copy of the detailed plan, with a listing of flowers chosen, and the cost involved, once you have paid the deposit.

Assign "deal with it" days
To keep from driving yourself and those around you crazy, assign "deal with it" days for the ensuing details of planning your wedding. Schedule these days strategically throughout the time between your engagement and the wedding. Arrange with your florist a date and time that you will contact them via phone for additional questions. Set up an appointment prior to the date of the wedding for finalizing details and paying the balance of the wedding. In the meantime, create an ongoing list of questions that occur to you and attach the list to your flower order. Deal with them on the assigned date of your phone call or appointment. Move anything that isn't completed on its "deal with it" day to a subsequent assigned date. Give yourself and others a break - don't dwell on the stress of completing tasks between "deal with it" dates.

Flower-Savvy Tip:
Use Smithers-Oasis® metallic or bouillon wire laced (or wound) around a stem of foliage as decoration or to made the stem bendable for designing purposes.

Ivy
Asiatic Lilies
Lily Grass

Develop a theme

How to Develop a Theme for Your Wedding

A bride who feels overwhelmed when planning a wedding, may find that working within a theme provides an easy guideline for making detailed choices. There are some simple, basic steps to take in planning a theme for your wedding.

Select a theme

Look to your own personalities, cultural background, ceremony setting, or a special shared interest as the inspiration for your wedding theme. Be careful to choose something that is more timeless than trendy so that you won't think it foolish in years to come. Make it equally intriguing to both of you. It can be as simple as featuring a favorite color, flower, or monogram. Or, it can be as complex as creating a scene from another time period, celebrating common heritage, or combining two different cultural backgrounds. Select a theme, then be sure it applies in each area of your plans.

Create the setting

Start with the most important scene - the two of you joining hands in marriage ... the "you may kiss the Bride!" moment... and work backwards when making your plans. What does the setting look like at that special moment in your mind? Bring your vision to life by compiling a detailed account of what the environment surrounding you looks like in your imagination. Seek a setting that will accommodate that scenario in real life. Envision the personalities, clothing, flowers, music, props, etc. necessary to create this scene. List the details it will take to develop your chosen theme in that setting. Then move forward in your thinking to the reception. What type of setting will you need for those festivities? List the components necessary such as food, music, tables, seating, décor, etc. to bring your vision to life. Use this combined outline of information as the beginning of your 'to do' list.

Sprengeri
Chrysanthemum Daisies
Smithers-Oasis® Apple Green Aluminum Wire

Tell a story

Think of your wedding day as one of the highlights of your own personal love story. Dramatize the story in your mind as though it were a scene in a fairy tale. Create a visual image or logo, color harmony, personal style or recognizable detail that can convey your message to your audience (guests) and help them share your romantic experience. Look for ways to repeat that one, clear message.

Embellish the detail

Follow through the details of the wedding telling your story. Start with the written word - 'save the date' cards, invitations, programs, menu cards, napkins, web site, thank you notes, etc. making certain that each reflects the theme. Do the same for each category that you must plan. For example, you want the flowers to represent the same look the food and music do. Careful attention to intricate detail will be noticed and appreciated by guests. Look for ways to convey your message in thoughtful details that add to their comfort. Send a gift of flowers or a guest snack bag to the hotel for travelers. Offer cups of coffee or hot chocolate 'to go' after a late evening of drinking and dancing. Give wedding mementos that help guests enjoy the festivities such as a ladies' wrap for a potentially cool outdoor evening event, or cold signature drink upon arrival at the reception on a hot summer day. All 'little extras' should reflect the theme of your wedding for continuity.

Five Steps for Developing a Theme for Your Wedding

- Select a theme
- Create the setting
- Tell a story
- Embellish in detail
- Inspire a memory

Cinco pasos para el desarrollo de un tema para tu boda

- Seleccione un tema
- Crear el establecimiento
- Cuenta una historia
- embellecer en detalle
- una memoria Inspírame

Flower-Savvy Tip:

Delicate flowers such as gardenias, stephanotis or lily of the valley can be covered with damp paper toweling inside the corsage bag to help keep them fresh and discourage browning.

When using flowers with little or no stem, such as gardenias, cymbidium or phalaenopsis orchids, clusters of hydrangea or stephanotis, snip the end of the stem and float the blooms in a bowl of lukewarm water for about 30 minutes to allow the flower to hydrate completely. Then, remove the blooms, drain on paper toweling, and wire and tape as needed.

Sprengeri
Daisy Chrysanthemums
9' Smithers-Oasis® Foam Garland

J

Inspire a memory

Look for ways that you can create an experience for your guests so that your wedding can be remembered as a very special event for them as well as for yourselves. For example, if you are in a locale where the coffee is a specialty and you serve it to your guests send coffee beans home with them as a wedding favor. As they grind the fragrant beans, they will be reminded of the wedding. Celebrating in wine country? Send along a bottle of wine that has been relabeled with a wedding label of your names and date. If it is to be a candlelight event, use candles of your favorite fragrance and send a similar candle home with each guest. Plan a post wedding breakfast or after rehearsal dinner party for traveling guests to extend the length of time they get to spend with you. For a small family wedding, give each relative a special duty in the on-site preparations. Appoint a family photographer to catch them doing their jobs on camera and later send them a copy of the photo along with your note of thanks. Make a donation to a charity of choice in the name of your guests in honor of the shared event. Think through the activities, rituals, or traditions that are important to your families and try to incorporate something of special meaning into your plans. Ask a family poet, vocalist, or cake baker, etc. to share their talent on that day. Including others thoughtfully in your wedding experience will make it more memorable for all of you.

Above all, once you have chosen a theme for your wedding be sure to keep the message consistent throughout all the wedding details.

Flower-Savvy Tip:

Flowers to be used in design work must be prepared, or processed, to achieve optimal freshness. Take each stem of flower and remove any unnecessary foliage for a better uptake of water. Be sure to remove leaves that would fall beneath the water line in your container as it will disintegrate and create bacteria in the water, shortening the life of the flower.

Storage buckets for flowers should be cleaned with hot water and detergent and rinsed thoroughly each time after use. To insure the flowers are placed in sanitary containers, the rule of thumb is that the bucket should be clean enough for one to drink from it.

Daffodils

Asiatic Lilies
Dusty Miller

Seasonal flowers

Select flowers that are in season
Selecting flowers that are in season and readily available can give a look of unity and be good for the budget as well. Seasonal flowers will coordinate with the color and style of the attire guests wear to the wedding. It can also be less stressful than ordering out of season flowers that are difficult to procure and are often more expensive. Look to nature for your inspiration of a natural mix of color and materials. If your event will take place in an outdoor setting this is especially important. Remember to consider the elements of shape and texture in your flower choice. Eye-catching shapes can add visual interest and the richness of texture is the luxury of design. Incorporate flowers that will add fragrance for an element of surprise. Along with adding beauty to the moment, fragrance can create a lasting impression; smell is the human sense that most often triggers memory. As you make these key decisions about the wedding's color palette and style your floral plan begins to take shape.

Flower-Savvy Tip:

To use large, fresh ivy leaves from your yard, cut and soak them in cool water until crisp. Drain water off. Mist individually with a foliage preservative and polish leaves with a drying cloth.

Ivy
Pansies
Snapdragons
Smithers-Oasis® Elegant Bouquet Holder

Working with spring bulb flowers

Although a favorite for spring arrangements, popular bulb flowers can create a unique challenge in design. Their soft, fibrous stems can be difficult to arrange in foam and can disintegrate in deep water. Also, tulips can grow in length overnight, altering the lines of a design.

To straighten tulip, mini calla or similar bulb flower stems, or to slow their opening, wrap snuggly in paper or cellophane wrapping while hydrating them in water. Or leave the dry, tightly wrapped bundle in refrigeration until just before use. This technique also works for other flowers such as peonies and iris. Tulip blooms will remain tight longer if ice cubes are placed in the water source to keep the stems cold. The blooms will often fully open when exposed to light and warmth. When in water fresh tulips can grow up to one and a half inches overnight causing them to lean and bend in unplanned directions. Be sure to anticipate these potential changes in your design concept. If you are not as pleased with this abundant look in your design perhaps it would be best to choose another flower.

To place hollow stems of spring bulb flowers into wet foam, insert a short wood pick or toothpick into the stem of the flower. Insert the wood pick and the flower stem into the foam making sure the stem connects to this water source. The wood pick will swell from the water and hold tightly in the foam. The cellulose, hollow stems of bulb flowers such as daffodils, tulips, gerbera daisies, miniature callas, etc. can deteriorate rapidly in water. Place stems in only 2-3 inches of water to prevent accelerated rotting in the vase. Be cautious of adding fresh flower food to the water source of iris as they can be chemically sensitive and fail to open.

To speed the unfurling of iris blooms, thump the side of a partially open iris with your finger to pop the bloom open. Re-cut the stem and place in cool water for added longevity. Pull back the green sheath of foliage at the base of the bloom to help it open.

Tulips
Smithers-Oasis® Silver Aluminum Wire

Bridal bouquet

Choosing your bridal bouquet

When choosing your bridal bouquet, give careful consideration to several aspects of your overall look. Consider your personal style, your body shape, and the lines of your dress when formulating the design of your bouquet. Be sure to address these issues with your florist during consultation. It is a good idea to offer photos and magazine pages that you have collected illustrating design styles and color harmonies that you especially like.

Consider your body shape

Your height should be the first consideration. Mention your height measurement to the florist as you discuss the length of your bouquet. Then consider your overall body shape. This should influence the shape and width of your bouquet.

For example, a petite bride should opt for a smaller bouquet that doesn't overwhelm or hide the dress. Small bouquets can be just as impressive as larger ones if they are interesting in detail. On the other hand, taller brides look very graceful holding a long, trailing bouquet. The newest trend in vertical bouquets can be an excellent choice for accenting this body type. A bride with a fuller figure might choose a larger bouquet that is rich in detail to capture the eye. A long, cascading design will flatter a full figure and lengthen her look by drawing the eye down instead of across the body.

Your choice of color harmony should also take into consideration the hue of your complexion, hair color and make up. Brides with dark complexion and hair can opt for a stronger floral color palette than a bride with fair skin and light hair color. Colors that are too bold can make a bride with a delicate complexion look too fragile. These factors should be taken into consideration when choosing the tone of your dress as well. Crisp whites are attractive on brides with a darker complexion and hair, while softer ivory tones highlight a bride with more delicate coloring. Adjusting your choice of make-up and accessories to fit your personal coloring and attire is important as well. If you are unsure of the appropriate colors, seek the advice of a professional makeup artist. Take all of these factors into consideration as you plan the color palette of your flowers for a coordinated look.

Ivy
Genestra
Roses
Oriental Lilies
Dendrobium Orchids
Foam Based Bouquet Holder

Consider the style of your dress

It is important to keep the cut and detail of a dress in mind when designing your bouquet so that the two compliment each other. Considering the style of your dress will help to determine your bouquet style. A traditional dress with a full skirt calls for a larger, more detailed bouquet for balance. A contemporary over the arm sheath or cuff bouquet cascading vertically would suit an elegant dress with a slim silhouette. A traditional cascade can accent the bodice of an empire waist, while a simple, casual dress is best accessorized with a small, informal bouquet. The traditional dress of a specific culture, of course, requires a bouquet that fits the same theme.

Equally important is the ornamentation of the dress. If your dress has many intricate details you will want to highlight those by using complementary detail in your flowers. If your dress is beautifully adorned, be careful not to allow the bouquet to overwhelm the dress with finishing details that are too busy, flowers that are too textural, or a size that is too large and hides the dress. Your florist will be able to help you select the most appropriate flowers to personalize your style, accessorize your dress, and complement your figure.

Provide the same basic information to your florist concerning your bridesmaids and their gowns. Offer estimations of height and body profiles, complexion and hair colors, and any special considerations for each girl. Provide a picture of the dress and color swatch, if possible.

Discuss the seasonal flower choices available for your bouquet. Ask for suggestions of appropriate substitutions should your first choices be unavailable. Realize that flowers are a perishable product and their availability can vary due to conditions that florists cannot control such as weather, transport, and quality issues. Decide with your florist on selections that reflect your choice of style, color, and textural preference. Agree on a price point for your bouquet and the bouquets for your bridesmaids, and place your confidence in their professional ability to make appropriate substitutions if necessary to provide you with a fresh, beautiful, well designed bouquet.

Assist your florist in designing your bouquet by taking to the consultation

- Picture or sketches and fabric swatches of your dresses
- Pictures of the bouquet styles that you prefer
- Samples of color harmonies you like
- Pictures of flowers that appeal to you
- Picture of your wedding day hairstyle if planning to wear flowers

Asiste al florista en el diseño de su ramo, llevandolo a la consulta

- Fotos o croquis y pedazos de muestras de tela de sus vestidos
- Fotos de estilos de ramos que usted prefiere
- Las muestras de armonía de color que tu prefieres
- Fotos de flores que atraen
- Fotos de su peinado el día de la boda , si la planifica llevar las flores

Hyacinths
White Feathers
#9 Organza Ribbon

Adding Personal Flowers

Bridesmaids

Bridesmaids are typically the closest friends of the bride or chosen family members of the couple. Their primary purpose is to provide support and assistance to the bride throughout the wedding process. As an honored member of the wedding party, bridesmaids get to spend the most treasured moments with the bride on her special day. Deciding on the number of bridesmaids is often challenging for the bride. Often, brides will select one bridesmaid per groomsman. As a rule of thumb, a more casual event will include less than a half dozen bridesmaids. A formal event can have up to a dozen bridesmaids. Five seems to be the favored number of bridesmaids for today's average wedding. The size of the venue where the ceremony is to take place and the size of your budget should both be considered when deciding how many attendants to include in your wedding party. Typically, more bridesmaids and groomsmen mean larger facilities, more guests, and therefore, more food and flowers. In general, adding to the number of bridesmaids adds to the expense of the wedding. If you are working within a tight budget, start managing costs by choosing a lesser number of bridesmaids.

Some brides choose to have all bridesmaids dress alike. Others prefer that the honor attendant dress differently. It is also popular for brides to allow bridesmaids to each wear different dress styles of the same color. Some brides choose one style of dress then vary the colors. In that same fashion, brides are also choosing to give each bridesmaid a different bouquet of flowers of a common theme.

Additional, honorary bridesmaids may be chosen, but as with ushers, they usually do not stand in the ceremony. They may be honored with flowers and escorted in by the ushers to a pew of honor behind the family pews prior to the processional. Flowers for bridesmaids and honorary bridesmaids are the expense of the bride as are the flowers marking their pew of honor.

Lily Grass
Oriental Lilies
Caladium Leaves
#9 Organza Ribbon

Corsages

After choosing the bride's and brides-maids' flowers, continue the plan with your choice of personal flowers. Having established your wedding color harmony and choice of flowers with the first bouquets, you can expand on that theme with subsequent corsages and boutonnieres. Ask each mother about her dress color in advance of the consultation. Provide a fabric swatch to the florist if possible. Traditionally, the mother of the bride chooses her dress first, selecting a color that harmonizes with the wedding scheme. The groom's mother then selects a dress of the same formality and a coordinating color. Grandmothers make their selections along the same guidelines. It has been common practice for the mothers to be presented a corsage of flowers similar to the blooms in the bridal bouquet. Grandmother's corsages can be similar, though a little less prestigious than the flowers of the moms. Another option is to order their corsages of flowers and buds that match the bridesmaid's bouquets. Typically, the groom provides the flowers for these women as they are the most honored guests of the wedding and therefore his special guests.

With today's popular fashion of simple dress styles often in delicate fabrics and sheer overlays, sometimes a pin-on corsage is too heavy and other options need to be considered.

Flower-Savvy Tip:

Gardenias are a popular and fragrant wedding flower. However, they will often turn a pale golden shade when exposed to light and warmth. Using floral preservative spays can help to some degree as a preventative. Be sure that you are just as pleased with this soft delicate color as you are their soft white fresh appearance, or perhaps it would be best to choose another white flower.

Bouvardia
Snapdragons
Hosta Leaves
Embroidered Linen Handkerchief

Flower options for Mothers

• A traditional shoulder corsage designed with flowers similar to the bridal bouquet.

• A wrist corsage of small flowers to be worn by each mother on her left wrist.

• A small nosegay or cluster of flowers that each mother can hold, giving her something graceful to do with her hands during photography. It is less likely to get bruised from hugging guests than a shoulder corsage, and can be laid at her place of seating during the reception.

• Tussie Mussie. A small ornate holder, usually in silver, that holds a small collection of flowers. Often these keepsakes can be engraved, kept as a family heirloom, and refilled with flowers at subsequent family weddings.

• Each mother may choose to carry a petite version of the flowers they carried on their own wedding day.

• A beautiful memento of the day for mothers and grandmothers can be a special piece of jewelry added to their coursage or bouquet as a keepsake. Search local flea markets for great finds in vintage jewelry.

• The stems of a posy or small nosegay of flowers can be wrapped in a monogrammed handkerchief and laced with ribbon to hold it in place. The handkerchief then becomes a personalized keepsake of the day.

• If they wear charm bracelets, engrave a charm with your names and wedding date and pin it into the flowers.

• Match a small evening bag to the dress of each mother, grandmother or other special guest and adorn with flowers. Give them on the day of the wedding as a memorable wedding gift. Or, if each mother has their own purse ask your florist to pin a simple corsage to it.

It is not required that each mother be presented the same flowers. However, the flowers should be of the same visual value. The shape and style can vary according to the preference of the recipient or the style of their dress. It is also permissible for the two mothers to be honored with one type of flower, such as a small posy to carry, while the stepmothers are presented with another style of flower, such as a shoulder or wrist corsage. In addition to wearing a flower, mothers, grandmothers, and other special guests are seated in pews of honor marked by bows, candlelight, or flowers.

Roses
Asiatic Lilies
Hypericum
6 Inch Gold Smithers-Oasis® Wire Collar

Boutonnieres

Groomsmen

Depending on the size and formality of the ceremony, groomsmen may function as attendants of honor or they may take the duties of ushers as well. In a smaller ceremony, a small group of men can perform both jobs. In a larger, more formal ceremony, additional ushers may be chosen for the purpose of seating guests, but not take part in the ceremony as do the groomsmen. After all guests have been escorted into the ceremony ushers may take a seat in the back of the ceremony or stand on either side of the wedding party. In general, it is a good idea to consider providing one usher per each fifty guests. If there are candles to light at the altar and the job hasn't been assigned to younger boys, two men from either group can additionally perform those duties.

Both groomsmen and ushers usually receive boutonnieres that are traditionally the expense of the groom. Their boutonnieres can either be designed the same or differently by group. The same applies to the boutonnieres for fathers, grandfathers, musicians, readers and clergy, which are also provided by the groom. The flowers chosen for groomsmen boutonnières usually coordinate with the bridesmaids flowers. They can consist of one main flower, or can be a small cluster of secondary blooms. Flowers chosen for fathers and grandfathers often match the mothers and grandmothers.

Blooms for the other participants may be chosen from any of the flowers used in the wedding floral collection or of the same color palette. Some brides choose to use bits of foliage as boutonnieres for a more masculine look.

Mini Philodendron 'Xanadu' Leaf
Yellow Rose
Lily Grass
Gold Bouillon Wire

Arranging your flowers

Arranging your own wedding flowers

Many brides think that the flowers are a good place to cut costs from the budget by arranging their own. Often this has disastrous results. Flowers are perishable and must be handled with care. They require a water source, refrigeration, and must be designed in the last hectic days prior to the wedding, when time is at a premium. It is best to consider this cost-cutting task only if you have close friends or family members who are trained in the art and can take over the responsibility of design, storage, delivery, set up, and removal for you. The bride and her mother should be free to spend the day together preparing to look their best for the celebration and enjoying the arriving guests. To be in the background working frantically before such an important event can be very stressful. You might be a great cook but you probably wouldn't want to spend your wedding day slaving in the kitchen; you may be very artistic, but you might not enjoy hauling buckets and boxes of flowers to the ceremony on your wedding day. I have personal experience in this area. As a floral designer at the time of my wedding, many years ago, I thought it very cool to design my own flowers, in addition to the money I thought I would save. It is easy to underestimate the amount of time preparing flowers will take. In the last hours before my wedding as I rushed home to quickly dress, I realized that perhaps there were other, more efficient, less stressful ways to work within a budget.

Flower-Savvy Tip:

If you get lily pollen on your clothing do not place water on the spot or it will create a stain. Use a chenille stem or scotch tape to lift off loose pollen. Place the article of clothing outdoors in direct sunlight. Leave it for about an hour and the pollen will evaporate without leaving a stain.

If you cut yourself while designing and get a blood stain on your clothing, pour hydrogen peroxide on it and the stain will evaporate. This technique can also be used on colored clothing.

Roses
Ornamental Mini Cabbage
Alstromeria
Succulent
Kermit Poms
Smithers-Oasis® Elegant Bouquet Holder

Summer
Summer, the living is easy, and weddings more casual

"When you decide to include children in your ceremony it is important to remember that you are doing just that - including children!"

Including children

When you decide to include children in your ceremony it is important to remember that you are doing just that - including children! It is unrealistic to expect them to act as miniature adults. A relaxed attitude and good sense of humor can save the day from disappointment if things don't go exactly as planned.

If you are concerned about the length of the ceremony for a younger child, it is appropriate for an older child to walk them down the aisle and then have the youngest sit with an adult on one of the front rows. If you have an unsure child who will stand during the ceremony, place them near an adult attendant that they feel comfortable with. Mark on the floor with a piece of tape the exact spot where you would like the children to stand.

Keep in mind that your guests will have an accepting, emotional response to participating children. Try to do the same. Let any imperfections in their role as flower girl, train bearer, or ring bearer become a funny personal story to tell in years to come instead of a source of disappointment. Relax and enjoy the pleasure of including your favorite children in this special time for your families.

Ivy
Roses
Zinnia
Dendrobium Orchids
Seeded Eucalyptus Buds
Smithers-Oasis® 6 Inch Silver Wire Collar
Beaded Garland

Floral suggestions for flower girls

- The most popular tradition for flower girls is to fill a small basket with petals that she can strew down the aisle before the bride. This is a beautiful part of the ceremony for a child old enough to confidently do so. However if a flower girl is very young, this can be a confusing job and lead to tears or retreat once it's time to descend the aisle and she is faced with all your guests watching her. Instead, fill her small basket with flowers and just let her carry it.

- If your bridal gown is being custom designed, consider using remnants of the gown material to cover a plain basket in layers of elegant material, coordinating the flower girl with the bride. Fill the adorned basket with either petals or flowers.

- If you were once a flower girl and still have the heirloom basket, recycle it by having your flower girl carry it down the aisle in your wedding.

- Another option is to give the flower girl something she can hold onto such as a tiny bouquet. If you have multiple girls, give each a different bouquet containing one variety of flowers that all tie in visually with the flowers carried by the bridesmaids.

- If the flower girl is very young have a simple wristlet made on a length of ribbon and tie it around her wrist. For an infant, glue a single flower head such as a daisy to a small circular band-aid and stick the band-aid to the wrist of the baby.

- If you have multiple flower girls or one or more are younger, consider having one long garland that each holds onto. This ropes them into one floral line as they descend the aisle. The youngest can be placed behind the oldest in line for easier manageability.

- A kissing ball, or floral pomander, is a great choice for a flower girl. The handle made of ribbon, velvet cording, or perhaps a decorative bead bracelet can be worn over the wrist of the small child with the ball of flowers hanging from it.

- A small wreath of flowers can have an engraved silver bell tied into it. The flower girl descends the aisle in front of the bride gently ringing the bell to announce the beginning of the formal ceremony.

- A small, fashionable purse left open and filled with flowers is fun for little flower girls to carry down the aisle.

Dendrobium Orchids
Smithers-Oasis® 8 Inch Gold Wire Collar

• For a garden wedding, glue long-lasting flower heads such as daisy mums randomly over the skirt of the flower girl's dress. Do this on the morning of the wedding for freshness. Complete the ensemble with a headpiece of fresh daisies.

• For a wedding on the seashore, send the flower girl barefoot down the sandy aisle carrying a large open seashell filled with flower petals to strew before the bride.

• Honor a deceased family member by incorporating a piece of her jewelry, such a pin or brooch, into the flowers of the flower girl.

• In a variation of the bride and groom giving a rose to their mother as a part of the ceremony, have two flower girls descend the aisle to present a rose to each mother. Be sure to wire the roses for extra strength to keep the children from snapping the head off.

Don't forget the headpieces to match

• Flower girls can look like small cherubs with garlands of flowers in their hair. Often their hair is very fine so carry a profusion of hair pins for pinning the floral halos in place. On a very young child, it sometimes works best to pin hair barrettes into their fine hair, then pin the headpiece to the barrettes.

• Floral halos made by hand wiring clusters of gypsophillia, also known as baby's breath, into a circlet are very popular. If you choose to lace with ribbon and add a bow for accent, consider tying tiny wisps of baby's breath into the streamers for love knots.

• Small garlands of flower heads such as spray roses or daisies wired together into a circular form and either left plain or adorned with a tiny bow and streamers are also a good choice for flower girls.

• Small flower heads can also be wired or glued into a hair barrette, fabric bow, or onto a headband for the flower girl to wear.

• For a garden wedding, a cute clutch or a summer hat pinned with a cluster of flowers gives a sassy look to the flower girl.

Flower-Savvy Tip:

When designing with flower buds that will not have a water source such as orchids in a hairpiece or vertical bouquet, dip the stem of the bloom in hot candle wax to sear the end, seal in moisture, and encourage longevity.

When packaging a headpiece, place numerous hairpins in the package so that they will be available when needed.

Creative ideas for ring bearers

• For the ring bearer pillow always use fake rings, never the real ones. Many horrified guests have watched helplessly as the bride's or groom's carefully chosen rings have fallen to the floor and rolled down a heat vent.

• Cover a small pillow, like a tooth fairy pillow or one of the small message pillows that can hang on a doorknob, with green moss. Tie a ribbon around it as though you were tying a package with a small bow at the top center. Tie a very small cluster of flowers and faux rings into the bow.

• Tie a ribbon around a small children's bible, favorite book of poetry, or other meaningful book as though you were tying a package with a small bow at the top center. Tie a tiny cluster of flowers and faux rings into the bow.

• Select a small elegant box that fits the theme of the wedding. Place a tiny cluster of mosses, flowers, and faux rings in the center of the box. Leave the box open so that the interior can be seen. Have the ring bearer descend the aisle carrying the box.

• New and interesting colorful metallic wires can be wound over and over around a satin pillow for an abstract look. Beads or pearls stranded on the wires can add visual interest. Accent with small clusters of flowers and faux rings to the top center.

• Have a small pillow made from the same fabric as the bridesmaids' dresses. Stitch a narrow strip of fabric or ribbon underneath the pillow for the child to insert their hand through to hold it. Monogram the center of the pillow and pin the faux rings there along with a single flower bloom.

• Choose a crystal or silver tray. Lay a monogrammed handkerchief in the center. Pin a small flower and faux rings onto the handkerchief.

• Select a very small but interesting piece of pottery and place the rings inside on a nest of mosses or flowers.

• Monogram a small silver bell and attach a small cluster of flowers and the rings to the base of its handle. Have the ring bearer enter the ceremony just before the bride, ringing the bell in the watchful silence to alert the guests to stand for her entrance.

• If the ceremony is near water, choose a large seashell and place inside of it small mosses and flowers with faux rings, attach the rings to a large starfish that the child can carry, or select a clear vessel to fill with sand, tiny seashells, and the rings placed in the center.

• If the ceremony is in a garden, fill the center of a small bird nest with mosses or berries and attach faux rings.

• If you want to include a (small) family pet in the ceremony, adorn the dog collar with flowers and faux rings and allow the ring bearer to walk it down the aisle by its leash.

• For a very young ring bearer, completely cover a small plush animal such as a teddy bear with mosses or simple flower heads like daisy mums and tie the faux rings to the bear's hand.

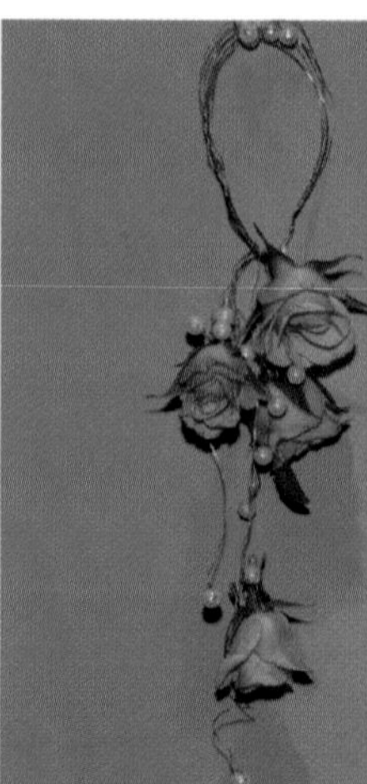

Spray Roses
Sprengeri
Amaranthus
Basket Base Removed
Large Smithers-Oasis® Bravo Holder

• If you would like to honor a deceased male family member, choose a personal item such as an old pipe or pocket watch and attach a small cluster of flowers and faux rings to the item. Have the ring bearer carry the item down the aisle.

If you are concerned about guests bringing their children to the wedding, provide a nursery with a paid attendant at the ceremony site. Enclose a special card in your invitation indicating the time and location of the available childcare and asking for an RSVP of those who will need care. Include a line item for the recipient to respond with the current age of the child to help you prepare adequately. If you have a wedding web site, include the time and place of the childcare area online. Include a photo and credentials of the babysitter that you have hired for parental reassurance.

At the reception, it can be a good idea to set up a children's table for miniature guests. Ask your reception venue to set up a smaller, shorter table and chairs. Cover the table with paper or paper linens that the children can draw on. Place a small packet of crayons with their name on it at each plate as a place card. As their guest favor, create a small bag of quiet time activities for each child to enjoy at the wedding and take home afterward. Create interesting centerpieces for them, by filling clear plastic containers with fun colorful snacks like goldfish, M& M's and gummy bears. Just for fun, you can go online and personalize the M&M's with your own names. These centerpieces serve as décor, entertainment, and dessert all in one. Order kid's meals for this table of small guests and save on food expense. Serve juice instead of champagne. Be sure to place the parents of these kids at tables nearby or have the paid babysitter from the ceremony sit with them during the reception as well.

Including children in your ceremony
Make it easy for the child to participate

- Give them responsibilities that are age appropriate
- Include them in only the last segment of the photo session
- Dress them in their wedding attire on site
- Offer them non-staining snacks and water to drink
- Provide them with a fun bag of quiet time activities
- Ask a parent to be with them at all times
- Have realistic expectations of the child

Incluidos los niños en su ceremonia
Hacer más fácil la participación de los niños

- Darles responsabilidádes que son adecuadas para la edad
- Incluir sólo en el último segmento de la sesión de fotos
- Vestirlos en el lugar de la boda
- Ofrecerles meriendas y refrigerios que no manchen la ropa
- Proveerles un bolso de actividades pasivas para momentos de silencio
- Pedirle a sus padre que esten con e los en todo momento
- Tener expectativas reales a los niños

102

Cymbidium Orchids
Hypericum
Roses

"Expense can grow quickly unless you take the time to carefully plan otherwise."

Going green

It makes 'cents' to think green

I recently realized that I had grown up green. However, in my family we referred to it as being sensible or living conservatively. It was a lifestyle of making the most of what you had available to you. The same concept can be applied to planning your wedding. It is so easy to get carried away when planning a wedding. Plans and expense can grow quickly unless you take the time to carefully plan otherwise. Set a budget and keep an accurate listing of actual costs as they are incurred. Consider taking these steps to cut costs and lessen the impact of your wedding on the environment and your bank balance.

Oriental Lilies
Gerbera Daisies
Roses
Ivy
Foam Based Bouquet Holder

Going green down the aisle

• Plan your ceremony close to home. Destination weddings are popular, but if most of your guests live near, staying in the area will decrease the carbon footprint that many guests traveling to a distant site would create.

• Select a natural site. Opt for an eco-friendly location such as a local garden, waterfront, or other natural setting. Decorate with plants and flowers that can be used or planted onsite later. Be sure to leave the area unchanged by your event.

•Buy local. Choose local vendors to work with for wedding services. Give guests wedding favors that are produced locally. Register for gift registries in local businesses.

• Register for Eco-Chic gifts. When creating your bridal registry of gifts, choose environmentally friendly appliances and products. Contact local artists such as painters or potters and ask to register with them for gifts. Ask hostesses of your bridal parties to request that guests bring unwrapped gifts to save on the use of paper, tape, and ribbon.

• Use heirloom items. Follow tradition, by wearing the wedding gown of your mother or other loved one or donate yours to a charity or church after your wedding. Select fresh flowers for your hair instead of a veil. Use an old cherished basket for the flower girl's petals. Choose vintage dresses for bridesmaids, and allow groomsmen to wear their own dark suits. Give vintage pieces of jewelry to your attendants as thank you gifts.

• Recycle and reuse. Use recycled paper for invitations, programs, menus, and thank you notes. Request that reusable vases, dishes, and eating utensils be used. Use washable linens. Ask the caterer to recycle in the kitchen.

• Ask for organic. Ask your florist and caterer about using organic flowers and food. If organic is unavailable, choose items that are in season locally rather than having to be shipped in from long distances. After the event, donate flowers to churches or hospitals and food to local charities.

• Think digital. Many photographers release their collection of wedding photos on a web site rather than duplicate proof books for families to view for ordering. Set up a wedding website in advance for listing your details of time, place, and activities. Give detailed travel information and driving directions on this site, using less paper for instructions.

Going 'green' down the aisle

- Plan your ceremony close to home
- Select a natural, eco-friendly site
- Buy from local vendors
- Register for eco-conscious gifts
- Use heirloom or repurposed items
- Recycle and reuse
- Ask for organic
- Think digital for photos, wedding info

Ir "verde" por el pasillo

- Planifique su ceremonia cerca de casa
- Seleccione lugares ecológicos que protejan el ambiente
- Busca proveedores locales para tus compras
- Registrate para que te regalen regalos el eco-amigables
- Utilice artículos reciclables
- Reciclar y reutiliza
- Pida productos orgánicos
- Piense en fotos digitales

Bouvardia
Mint
Roses
Smithers-Oasis® Elegant Bouquet Holder

Oriental Lilies
Roses
Ivy
Foam Based Bouquet Holder

Snapdragons
Ivy Leaves

Destination wedding

With elaborate, expensive formal weddings becoming more popular, some brides are opting instead to celebrate with smaller more intimate groups of family and friends at faraway destinations. This allows them to celebrate their wedding in less formal surroundings than the traditional church sanctuary filled with hundreds of acquaintances. By choosing to limit the guest list, some brides feel they can more easily manage their budget. Planning the wedding ceremony for a remote location that guests must travel to automatically lessens the number of attendees. If travel isn't an option for your family, another way of minimizing the number is by selecting a local setting that can only accommodate a small number. If the cost still exceeds your budget, another means of cutting back is to have a private ceremony with a larger reception. A smaller guest list can help keep the budget under control yet still be a memorable event for the bride and groom and their immediate families.

B

Budget your expenses

If you are considering a destination wedding primarily as a means of cutting costs, you must keep your budget in mind throughout the planning process. Run through the weekend in your mind listing events that you might want to incorporate into a wedding itinerary. Calculate projected costs for each activity. Along with the obvious costs of travel and lodging remember to incorporate the expense of creating travel information packets, weekend itineraries, local sightseeing tours, maps, guest room gift baskets, etc. into your projected budget as these unseen expenses can add up quickly. Carefully assess your travel expenses, facility fees, and resort prices for meals, flowers, alcohol, etc. to be sure that a destination setting is actually less expensive. Get an itemized projection of all costs in writing in advance to study before signing any contracts. Calculate the difference between a local and distant setting.

Consider others

You and your fiancé should sit down with parents for an honest discussion of the pros and cons for your families of planning a destination wedding before making your final decision. Make a list of the guests that you really want to spend your special day with and analyze each name, considering health and expense, in order to venture a guess as to whether or not it is feasible for them to join you. Be sure to tell your wedding party of your plans and their projected costs before asking them to commit to participating in your wedding.

Hire a professional to help

For a young professional with a busy career, saving money isn't always the issue. An intimate destination wedding handled via the internet and phone calls can be less stressful than attending to the endless details that a large traditional church wedding and reception can entail. Once the location has been chosen it becomes easy to build a theme with the choice of dresses, flowers, food, and music that will express the ambiance of the location. Typically, a destination wedding is more relaxed as guests are more accepting of details gone awry. In an effort to help make your plans go more smoothly, it is wise to ask if the resort has an on-site wedding consultant or can recommend a local wedding specialist to you. The sage advice of a local who can handle advance details and help you to secure the services of local vendors can be invaluable. Ask if the consultant will also be available to your guests for pre-planning their trips. If not, ask them to refer a local travel agent or hotel concierge that your guests can contact for advice.

Visit the location

Once your plans are underway, visit the site if possible to interview potential vendors and see the facilities. Ask to see photos of their work and a list of referrals from previous brides. Collect as much information as possible about the area for your guests. Meet with your wedding planner and finalize as many details as possible. Take home many photos, site drawings, menus, and a detailed contact list to make subsequent decisions easier to manage. Once you have established your itinerary, send out "save the date" cards to friends and family so that they too can begin their plans.

Create a resource of information

Well in advance of the wedding, gather all the pertinent information you can in order to assist your guests in planning their own schedules including travel, hotel, restaurants, and local activities. Secure printed brochures and price sheets or web site addresses and phone numbers that provide them with the necessary information regarding options and costs. Set aside a block of rooms in a hotel and give your guests the wedding code and final booking date. Remind

Planning a destination wedding

- Budget your expenses
- Be considerate of cost for others
- Hire a professional to help
- Visit the location
- Create a resource of information
- Finish handling all details before leaving home

La planificación de una boda de destino

- Presupuesto de sus gastos
- Ser considerado de los costos de otros
- Contrate a un profesional para ayudar
- Visita el lugar de la actividad
- Crear un listado de recursos
- Finalizar el manejo de todos los detalles antes de salir de la casa

Flower-Savvy Tip:

When using floral bouquets in hot temperatures keeping them cool is important. If easy access to refrigeration is unavailable, keep large ice coolers available for storage to maintain freshness. Layer the bottom of the ice chest with bags of ice and layer with newspaper or thin toweling. Cover with a thin sheet of plastic and lay the bouquets on top.

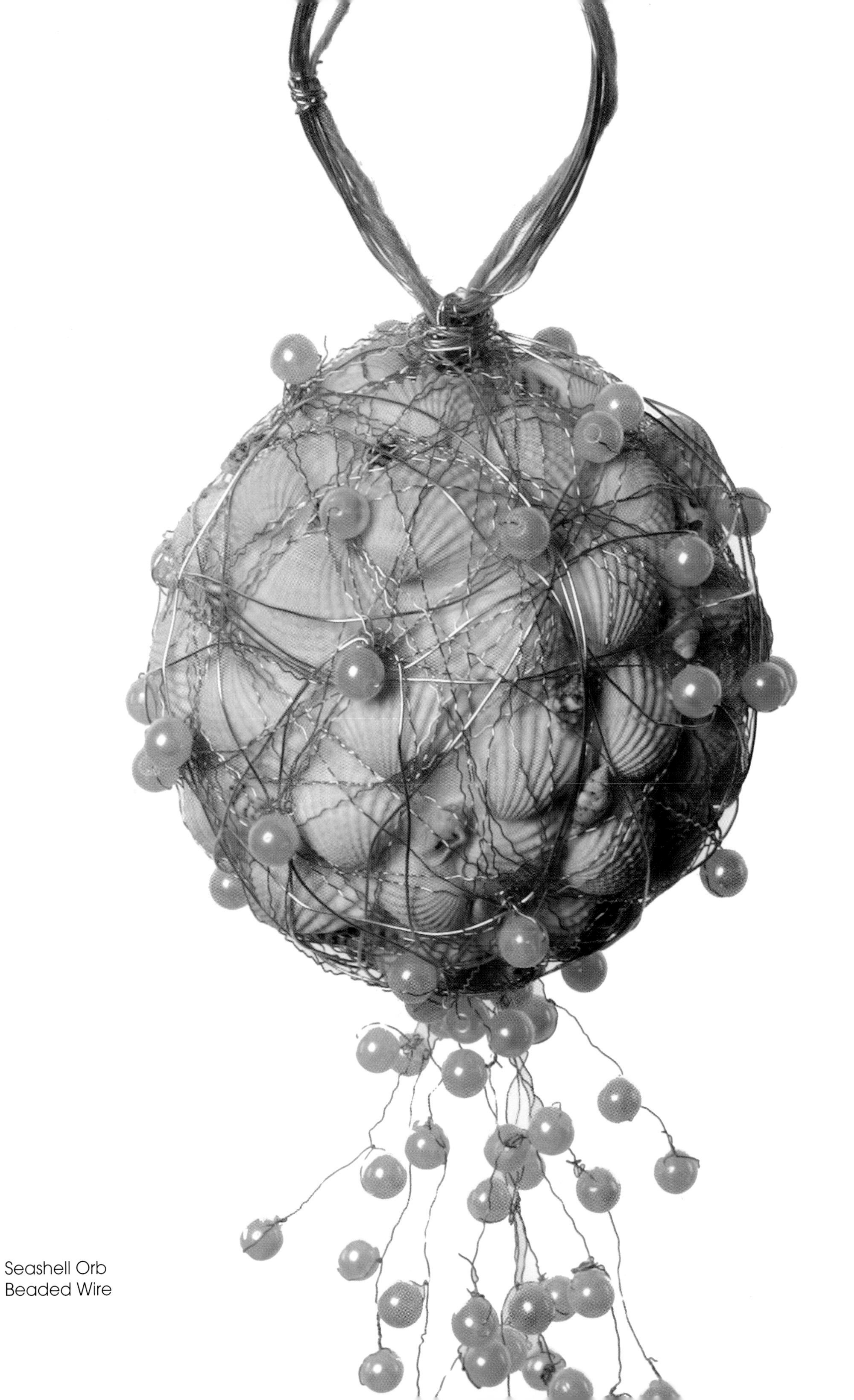

Seashell Orb
Beaded Wire

guests to arrange in advance travel to and from the airport. Put all the details together into one informative packet that you can give to guests as they make their plans. Provide plenty of contact numbers so that they can make their own arrangements and you don't have the added stress of becoming their travel agent. If expense is an issue, consider creating your own wedding web site with all this information for an easy and cost-effective way of informing your guests. Be sure all your potential guests are tech savvy, or you may need to provide some with printed materials.

Finish before you fly

Take care of all time-consuming details such as locating room assignments, developing wedding itineraries, creating seating charts, and making place cards before leaving home. If you plan to have a hospitality suite for guests to use to meet and mingle, gather all the refreshments for it as soon as you arrive. Have all weekend plans complete and take your organizational file detailing the commitments of various vendors with you for backup. The wedding weekend is for celebrating and enjoying time with your guests, not finishing your tasks.

Flower-Savvy Tip:

For an interesting bouquet handle cover, wrap and adhere ribbon to the stem and handle of the plastic bouquet holder and secure in place. Slide a Fitz design pearl wristlet over the handle and up onto the base of the holder as a decorative cover. Glue in place.

Delphinium
Gerbera Dasies
Seeded Eucalyptus Buds
Foam Based Bouquet Holder

Your signature style

From beginning your plans to implementing the last details it is important that you organize your wedding in your own signature style. While it is wise to listen to the seasoned advice of wedding professionals, always remind them that you want the end result to reflect your personality. What is your signature style? It is the look or expression of personal taste that defines 'you' to others.

A wedding is truly 'your' day. This is the perfect opportunity to make a visual statement on how you will evolve in this new stage of life. Personal style is an attitude, an enthusiasm for things that you love, an instinctive knowledge that your choices matter. Showing confidence in your signature style signals others that you know who you are, what you like, and are comfortable with your choices.

How can you develop your signature style?

• Define yourself

Look for inspiration in the things you surround yourself with. Select your favorite colors, fashions, flowers, accessories, and music to reflect your personal taste. Choose something you love versus just following current trend or fashion. Be your own wedding fashionista and showcase a look that is truly you. If you already have a defining signature look, blend it into your wedding selections so that the day will reflect your personal style.

• Decide on your statement

Determine what you want to accomplish and create more impact by focusing on that goal rather than blending a clutter of looks and ideas. Do you love hats? Include them in your wedding wardrobe and choose hats for the bridesmaids as well. Have a penchant for vintage clothes? Consider vintage dresses for your bridesmaids and vintage jewelry for your thank you gifts. Love romantic, feminine looks? Create a wedding plan that highlights pastel colors, soft draping fabrics, delicate writing materials, and a light menu of refreshments. Above all, choose a look that you enjoy.

See yourself in the spotlight

Picture yourself as the focus of attention for that day. Make sure that the setting, fashion, décor and planned events all fit your personality, and that you are comfortable with them. Nothing is more noticeable than an uncomfortable bride who is going through the motions of trying to meet someone else's expectations of how things should be. Actually, what this *should* be is a day of happiness that reflects the way you choose to express yourself.

Asiatic Lilies
Hydrangea
Solidago

M

Make it memorable

Accessories, props, and decorations can help to complete the look, but be careful not to overdo it. Subtle details can speak just as fluently of your signature style without overwhelming your guests. Keep all elements in balance for a unified look. For example: if you love classic styling – select an elegant, monochromatic theme. Choose dresses with simple, flowing lines and place a mass of fresh lilies in urns atop Grecian columns.

Include traditional flowers of formality such as orchids, roses, gardenias, stephanotis, or lily of the valley for personal flowers and stylized bouquets.

Express your personal taste with confidence; enthusiasm is contagious. If you show excitement in the planning of details for your wedding - using your signature style, your guests will share in the pleasure of 'your' special day with you.

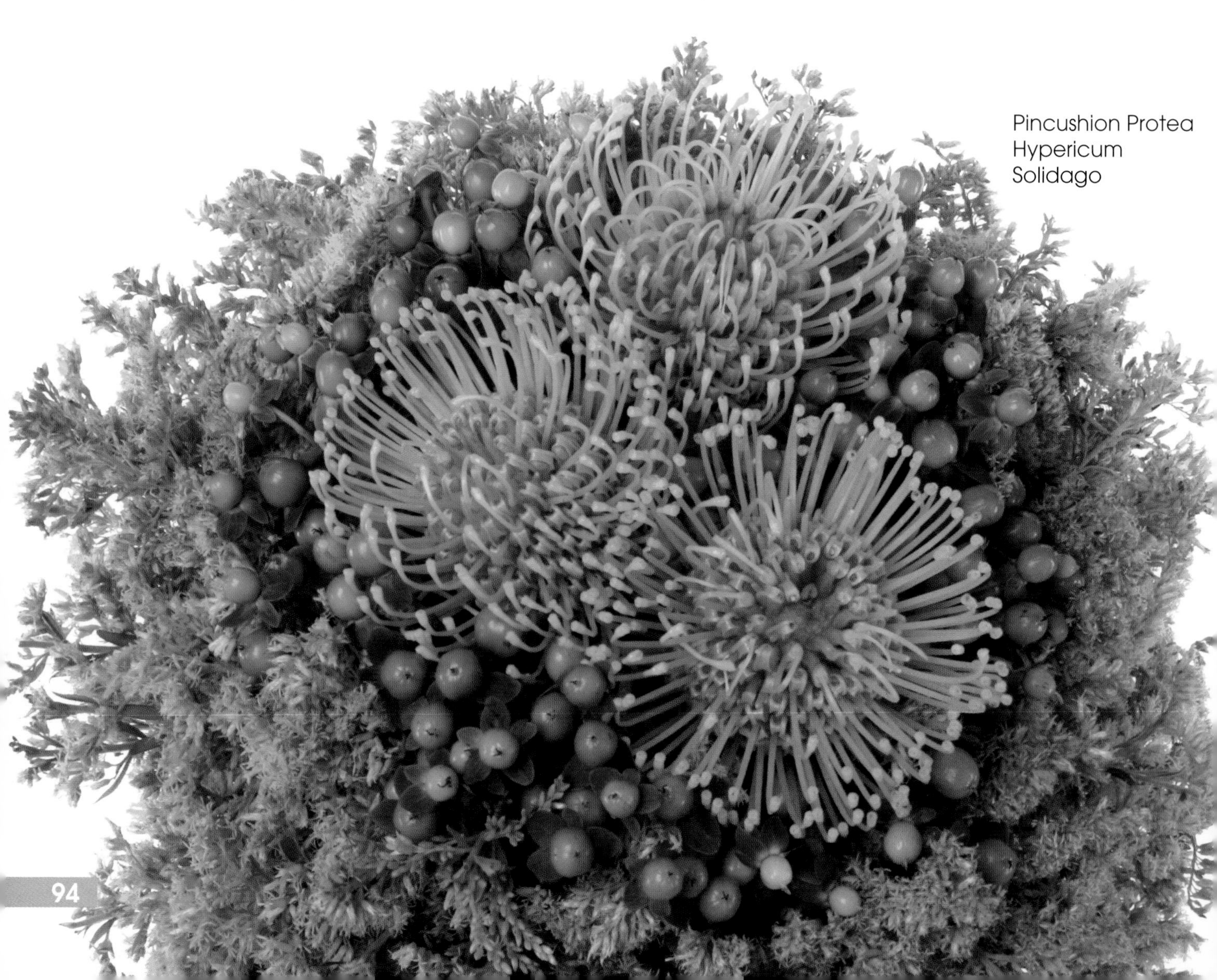

Pincushion Protea
Hypericum
Solidago

Ivy
Alstromeria
Hydrangea
Yarrow

Flowers for your cake

Fresh flowers are a popular choice for wedding cake décor. If possible, provide your florist with a photo or diagram of the cake you have selected during your consultation. This will help them in calculating the volume and price of flowers needed. Give the florist and cake baker each the contact information of the other. Ask that they schedule in advance a time to meet on-site to decorate the cake. As a precaution, ask that they exchange cell phone numbers in case of a cake emergency.

One decorating technique that works well is to have the cake baker place mounds of icing in the areas where the florist will insert fresh flower stems. The icing acts as the design mechanic that holds the flowers in place without the stems touching the edible parts of the cake. The florist can mark the spots for the placement of icing mounds on the diagram or meet the cake baker on-site for the cake installation. Or, the cake baker can leave a tube of icing and the florist can place the mounds as they design. Prior to cutting and serving the cake, a cake server can be used to remove the flowers and icing to a plate nearby.

Flower-Savvy Tip:

Add family heirlooms to the table. Use your parents framed photographs from their weddings to add décor to the table. Further enhance this display of family treasure by adding each mother's veil or place their wedding gown on a dress-making bust on either side of the table.

Sweetheart table

While a sweetheart table seems like a romantic gesture, it can also be a matter of practicality. This typically small round table is for the bride and groom only at the reception. This is convenient for a couple who have divorced parents in attendance so they don't have to choose between parents when it comes to seating; the same applies to choosing between friends or bridal party. The couple can circulate the room greeting guests while bridesmaids and groomsmen are freed from the head table and can enjoy sitting with their escort or family. When the couple is seated alone at their personal table, guests feel more comfortable approaching them than at the center of a ceremonial head table. It is important, however, that the sweetheart table be placed inclusively among the guests. To place it exclusively above or aside from the guests will make the newly wed couple seem inhospitable and unapproachable.

The sweetheart table doesn't require much decor as the table itself only seats two people. Suggestions include:

- A smaller version of the centerpieces used on the guest tables.
- A centerpiece that reflects their honeymoon destination.
- A vase placed on the table that the bridal bouquet can be placed in as the centerpiece.
- A collection of various heights of candles that will highlight the faces of the happy couple.
- A miniature wedding cake just for two made of their favorite types of cake.
- A bubble bowl filled with flowers and goldfish which are a symbol of good luck.
- A sheath of wheat adorned with flowers as a symbol of good luck and fertility.
- Decorations placed on the backs of the chairs indicating seats of honor.

Flower-Savvy Tip:

When processing roses, remove leaves from the stems leaving only one or two leaves at the top, just beneath the bloom. Clip thorns from the stem without cutting into the flesh of the stem. Leaving one or two leaves and not making gashes in the stem will help insure that water travels all the way up to the bloom. Cut on the diagonal - a good sharp cut, and place into 5" – 7" of warm water. Add flower food.

If a rose develops bent neck – where the still tight bloom has wilted over unopened, give the stem end a sharp diagonal cut and submerge the entire rose in warm water. Leave it there until the water cools or you can see the stem firm and straighten.

Roses
Genestra
Alstromeria
Hydrangea
Variegated English Ivy
Foam Based Bouquet Holder

Planning outdoor events

Planning an outdoor event requires more attention to detail than using an indoor site. In addition to people, place, and things you also have to consider temperature, wind, and rain. Doing your homework in advance is important when making your plans.

Consider the weather

If you are planning to have an outdoor event, it is a good idea to look at long-range weather forecasts prior to setting the date. One valuable source of information is the Farmers' Almanac. This resource of projected weather forecast is usually about 80 – 85% correct. I encourage brides to consult it as a part of their pre-planning research. Sometimes the expected weather may vary by a couple of days or its intensity may fluctuate, but it is accurate enough that I would not recommend planning an outdoor event when inclement weather is suggested. The Farmers' Almanac has been printed yearly since 1818 and projects the weather in monthly increments for seven distinct regions of the country. Brides can check the date they are considering in the region they hope to be married in and get an overview of the type of weather that can be expected. Copies of the Almanac are usually available for less than $10 in the magazine section of many drug stores, newsstands, and mass merchandisers. It can also be ordered online at www.farmersalmanac.com.

Plan for the comfort of your guests

Ultimately, your guests are the reason for having a ceremony. If your plans didn't include guests, the two of you could easily arrange things more simply. Since you do wish to say vows in front of your loved ones you should take the time to be considerate of their comfort. Consider your chosen site from a guest's point of view. Is there adequate seating? Will their seats be too hot, cold, or windy? Will they be able to see the ceremony well from their seats? Will they be facing into the sun? Will they have difficulty reaching the site? Is there adequate and available parking? Be considerate of your guests as you plan and think from their point of view.

Think of how temperature will affect foods and plan accordingly.
If facilities allow, it is sometimes easier to celebrate wedding vows outdoors and return indoors for serving food to your guests. Keeping food safe in extreme heat or palatable in very cold weather can be difficult outdoors. In addition to the concerns of temperature, insects may also be a problem. Ask for the advice of your caterer about the serving safety and presentation of your foods. Carefully consider the flow of your event not only in beautiful weather but in inclement weather and adjust your plans accordingly.

Take precaution against insects
Being besieged by insects can rob the joy of attending an outdoor event for guests (not to mention you). Be sure to consider the invasion of insects during your ceremony and take precautions in advance. Ask your facility wedding planner or host to help take steps to alleviate the attendance of unwanted pests. Bug sprays, granular repellants, citronella candles, and Tiki torches might help if utilized in advance and during the ceremony.

Use flowers of the season
Flowers of the season are often more prepared for the current outdoor temperature than flowers of another season or those grown in another locale or climate. For example, delicate spring flowers grown from bulbs are less prepared for surviving intense heat than perennial wildflowers blooming in deep summer. In addition, to a financial savings of using flowers that are readily available in the season, the flowers are accustomed to the temperatures of that season. Typically, the color of seasonal flowers is complimentary to the fashion colors of the season as well.

Flower-Savvy Tip:
Create a list of names of wedding participants along with their job descriptions and provide a copy to your florist and wedding director. Ask your florist to label each design (corsage, bout, etc.) with the appropriate name. The director can then utilize the labeled items to easily distribute flowers to participants.

If transporting hand-tied bouquets in vases of water, add ribbon on-site to keep it from getting wet. If this is not possible, consider using organza ribbon as it sheds water and dries quickly.

Curly Willow
Bear Grass
Lily Grass
Oriental Lilies

List manner of dress on invitation

Guests will be more comfortable as they enjoy the festivities when dressed for the occasion. Be sure to indicate the manner of dress that is appropriate to the location on your invitation. In particular, footwear may make a difference if guests have to walk to reach your selected site. Old-fashioned handheld paper fans with the facility or couple's photo and wedding program printed on each side might be applicable for hot weather. Also consider the need for fire pits and warm drinks if the weather is cool. If the location is fairly warm, but can become cool once the sun sets, a wrap such as a pashmina or decorative scarf tied to reception chairs makes a great wedding favor for guests. If possible visit your site in advance, during the season and time of day of your wedding events, and carefully consider the comfort of your guests in terms of seating, eating, and temperature during that time.

Have a backup plan

When planning an outdoor event create a backup plan for indoor facilities in case of inclement weather. Check the extended weather forecast during your wedding week to keep updated as to potential weather situations. Advise your wedding party and immediate family of any alternate plans should weather situations arise. List the planned details of your alternate site on written information provided to the guests. For a small gathering, you might set up a chain of contact for reaching your guests with updated information regarding last minute changes. Provide your network of wedding professionals with all the information necessary for making sudden changes in location due to inclement weather as well.

Planning Outdoor events
Consider the weather

- Plan for the comfort of your guests
- Be careful of food in hot & cold temperatures
- Take precaution against insects
- Use flowers of the season
- List manner of dress on the invitation
- Have a backup plan

Planificación de eventos al aire libre
Considere las condiciones del tiempo

- Plan para la comodidad de sus invitados
- Toma precauciones con los alimentos de calor y Frios
- Toma precauciones contra los insectos
- Usar flores de temporada
- Lista de manera devestir en la invitación
- Tener Siempre un plan B por seguridad

Flower-Savvy Tip:

The best time to gather outdoor flowers or foliages to use in design work is early in the morning and in the evening. There will be less heat from the sun at those times of day resulting in flowers that are crisp and less dehydrated. Immediately process flowers, by removing foliages, cutting the stems with a sharp diagonal cut, and placing them in 5" – 7" of warm water that has flower food added. Foliages should be washed and sealed in a large plastic bag along with damp paper toweling for refrigeration. Spray with an anti-transpirant.

If onsite designing results in a dull knife and you don't have an available sharpener, run the blade of the knife through a piece of wax candle numerous times to make the blade cut easier.

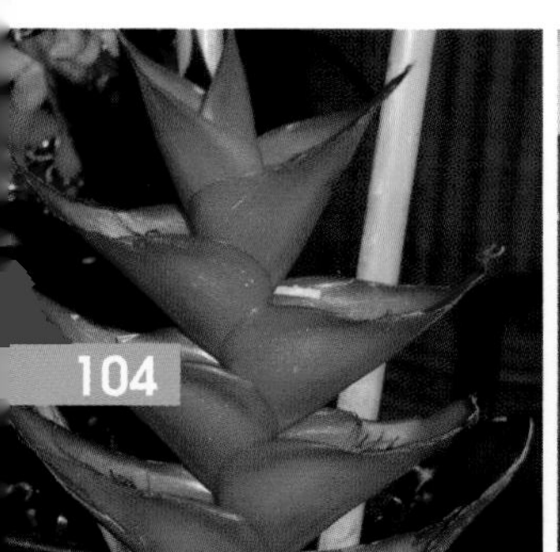

BANROCK
STATION

Working within a budget

Set your budget

Begin by determining the amount you can afford to spend on your wedding. Speak honestly with those who will contribute to covering the costs and determine an amount that you can all agree on. Divide this amount into the categories of expense. A wedding spreadsheet is a great way to list expenses and itemize costs. As you make purchases, note every expense.

Prioritize expenses

Prioritize your most important areas. Create a secondary list of 'wish' items that you hope to include, if funds are available. When working with a tight budget every expense must be considered and prioritized.

Keep all areas in balance

Write out your budget, dividing it between all areas equally. Recognize that if you plan to overspend in one area you will have to subtract from another. Keep in mind, that spending too much money in one area and not enough in another will not produce a harmonious effect. No one area of expense should overwhelm others. If you have the ability to save in one section then you can invest that savings in another category. For example, if your family owns a florist or your mom designs and sews your gown, that savings can be invested elsewhere. The key to a unified and harmonious look for your wedding is keeping the expense, formality and presentation of all areas of expense in balance.

Coleus
Mixed Nuts

Consider cost effective facilities
To determine your facility needs, consider the number of guests you will need a site to accommodate. Anticipate the amount of food, flowers and other décor that will be required for that site. Ask major questions relating to costs, concerning less expensive food options, provision of chairs, tables and linens, tableware and serving items. Can you provide your own alcohol? Is there gratuity expected? Outline your needs and ask for an estimate.

A site that is too large for a small number of guests, or a site too small for a large crowd can lead to greater expense. Choose a setting that fits the size of your guest list and keeps the budget in line.

Keep invitation list small
Key to keeping the numbers down is to select a small number of attendants. The number of attendants you choose will ultimately influence the number of guests, amount of flowers, food, beverage and space required for your event. To lower costs, choose a small wedding party.

Use your creativity
Diligently working within a budget can inspire you to be more creative. Explore ideas that use the combined talents of your friends and family. If you have a special talent, barter your services in advance for professional services on your wedding day. Budget-conscious couples may ask for wedding gifts of assistance rather than traditional gifts. Outline your plan of specific needs. Post it on your website or provide copies to your parents and honor attendants. Potential gift-givers can contribute to a wedding fund rather than giving a gift at the bridal shower. For example, a relative who loves flowers might donate to the flower budget. A favorite aunt who loves to bake might offer to create your wedding cake as her gift. These thoughtful gifts provide a non-traditional way to help budget-watching couples cut costs.

Working within a tight budget
- Set your budget
- Prioritize expense
- Keep all areas in balance
- Consider cost effective facilities
- Keep invitation list small
- Use your creativity
- Adopt cost-cutting measures

Trabajo dentro de un presupuesto ajustado
- Determine su presupuesto
- Priorizar gasto
- Mantener el equilibrio en todos los ámbitos
- Considerar rentable instalaciones
- Mantenga lista de invitados pequeña
- Use su creatividad
- Adoptar medidas de reducción de costes

Adopt cost-cutting measures
Consider using heirloom items from family weddings of the past such as borrowing Mom's dress, (altered to fit), using a borrowed veil or flower girl basket, etc. Suggest that men wear suits instead of tuxedos. Cut food costs by scheduling the reception at a time when a meal is not expected. Choose a color for the bridesmaid's dresses, then allow them to wear one they already own or buy one off the rack – with your final approval, of course.

Develop a 'help' list of chores that family and friends can choose from. Cash strapped loved ones might appreciate the opportunity to volunteer their help for an afternoon, or give their professional advice to you as their gift. A written 'I owe you' is a gift of help, fun and fellowship, and can be most valuable to both the new couple and gift givers in a cash crunch. Be sure to show your appreciation just as you would a gift that was purchased. Careful planning can benefit all when working within a tight budget.

Roses
Hydrangea
Hypericum
Seeded Eucalyptus
Gerbera Daisies
Wax Flower
Ivy Leaves
Hurricane Globe
9″ Pillar Candle-Ivory

Autumn

Cool
crisp
autumn
days
inspire
warm
colorful
displays

Planning a wedding at home

Weddings are a special celebration of life shared with family and friends. Events planned at home can be especially warm and inviting. Some brides choose to celebrate at home for sentimental reasons. For other brides it is cost-effective, as not paying a facility fee to have it elsewhere is helpful with a tight budget. Regardless of why you decide to have your wedding at home, there are a few steps that can help to make the day run a little more smoothly.

Develop a written plan
Sit down with all involved parties and write out a plan of details. Make a list of necessary tasks and assign them to members of the group. Start a master list of contact names, addresses, phone numbers, and email addresses for your network of organizers and vendors and make copies of it for everyone.

Schedule deadlines
Make out a schedule including deadlines for accomplishing all organizational tasks well in advance. Plan for your wedding details to be fully organized at least one week in advance or a month in advance, if at all possible. This will diminish your stress and allow your family to enjoy the pre-wedding time together.

Create a flow chart
Select a ceremony site in the home that allows plenty of space for guests to

Flower-Savvy Tip:
Tall, hard to wash glass cylinders can be easily cleaned with an Alka-Seltzer tablet dropped into water within the container. The foaming action will help clean the glass.

Asiatic Lilies
Gerbera Daisies
Kermit Poms
Roses
Hypericum
Curly Willow
Smithers-Oasis® Elegant Bouquet Holder

gather for the exchange of vows. Position food and beverage stations throughout the house to create a flow of guests from one area to another. Remember to accommodate for water or electrical needs. Rearrange furnishings when necessary to accommodate guests.

Make a back-up plan

If any of your ceremony takes place outdoors, it is important to make an alternative plan as a back-up in case of inclement weather. Check the weather in advance in the Farmer's Almanac at www.almanac.com or by purchasing a copy of the yearly magazine which is available at most local drugstores. Include the alternate plans in the invitation to guests if it requires relocating to another site.

Hire professionals when you can

While staying within your budget, hire as many wedding service professionals such as the caterer, landscaper, or table and linen rentals as you can to make the event less overwhelming for the family. Hire servers and additional kitchen help to make the event go more smoothly. Schedule times for installation and removal well in advance.

Delegate when possible

This is an important time to ask for help from friends and family, setting a timeline for each task. Select two or more hosts and hostesses from each family to help with greeting and directing guests. Identify each with a boutonniere or corsage so that guests will know to come to them with questions. They can also be depended upon in case of emergency.

Kale
Zinnias
Montbretia Blooms & Pods
Cotton Lace Ribbon

Create visual interest

Eye-catching designs can create visual interest to add to the celebratory nature of an event. Use the unexpected to capture the eye. Choose unpredictable forms such as tropical flowers in an English garden setting or flowers under water in glass on a tabletop. Place flowers in unusual settings: marking an entrance, decorating the restrooms, hanging from a chandelier. Select complimentary colors rather than coordinating colors to enliven a space.

• Make an ice champagne bucket to hold the bottle of champagne for the bridal toast. Use a plastic container that can be cut away from the design once it is frozen. Freeze fresh flowers and decorative accents in layers adding more water and items to each frozen tier. At the halfway point insert a second plastic container that will hold the space for the bottle. Fill this container with something heavy like rocks to weight it down and keep it in place. Finish filling up the outside container with water and flowers. This design should be made days in advance. Keep frozen until time for your event.

• Use a Styrofoam® ring or Oasis® sculpting sheet to float a flower arrangement in the pool. Anchor the design with a weight tied to fishing line to keep the water jet current from pushing the design to the side of the pool.

• Group a variety of colored glass vases, pottery, or metal containers in the center of a table and fill each with flowers of different varieties. Use a collection of bud vases and fill each with a single stem of a flower.

• Choose unusual items to use as the floral containers such as hats, hat or jewelry boxes, small interesting shopping bags, or something that pertains to the honoree's career or hobby.

• At a seated meal such as the rehearsal dinner or bridesmaid's luncheon - place a garland of greenery along the center of the table and insert framed childhood photographs of the bride and groom facing guests on both sides. Tuck fresh flower blooms in to add color and texture. Votive candles can be added if it is an evening meal.

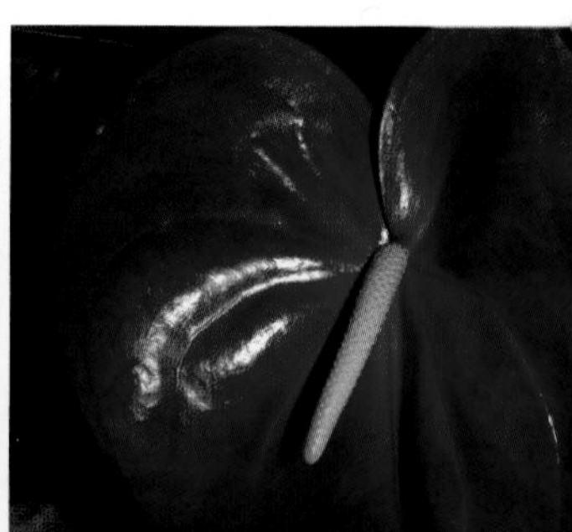

Zinnias
Celosia

IN HONOR OF
STEVENS

Gerbera Dasies
Ivy

Designing with callas

Callas and mini callas are often requested by brides as a favorite for their wedding bouquets and centerpieces. The calla's long stately stem and conical shaped bloom makes an interesting visual statement in floral designs. Callas are available in white, green, and yellow in the larger varieties. Miniature callas have a smaller, shorter stem and a bloom of lesser size. They are available in white, rose pink, yellow, lavender, deep purple, dark red, and a variety of bi-color blends. Colors and sizes available may vary with the season.

One interesting way to use callas is to create dramatic line in a design. Callas have a soft, fibrous stem that can be flexed when the fibers are broken. To do this, lay the calla on a table and let it come to room temperature. Or soak it in a bath of warm water to soften the stem tissue. Run your index finger down the length of the stem pressing on the spine to break down the inner tissues. This will allow you to bend the calla to conform to the shape of your design and attach it in place. Once the stem is re-hydrated or placed in refrigeration to become cold and crisp again, it will retain the shape that you have formed it into. When designing with, or storing callas in a vase, place the calla stems in a minimal amount of water. Calla stems quickly break down and turn to mush creating perfect conditions for bacteria and cutting the life of the flower. With less water, this is less likely to happen.

Flower-Savvy Tip:

Open-cut callas are cut in the field while the bloom is fully opened as opposed to the typical method of cutting callas before the bloom unfurls. Gathering and transporting open callas requires more care than greener cuts, resulting in higher costs. To create a faux open cut calla – completely submerge an unfurled calla stem in warm water. Once the bloom has softened, gently fold back the sides of the bloom and gingerly stuff moistened cotton balls or tissue into the bloom to hold it open. Give the end of the stem a sharp diagonal cut and place upright in 5" – 7" of warm water. Allow the bloom to dry; then remove stuffing material. The faux open calla bloom should hold its open shape.

Calla
Sedum
Celosia
Spray Roses
Zinnia
Solidago
Plumosa
Foam Based Bouquet Holder

Pincushion Protea
Delphinium
Mini Calla
Montbretia
Hydrangea
8 Inch Smithers-Oasis® Wire Collar
Smithers-Oasis® Iglu - Small

Make an entrance

Some little girls dream of their wedding all through their childhood. A favorite imaginary moment for this little future bride is the thought of descending the aisle to meet her groom at the altar. An abundance of fresh flowers lining the pathway is the perfect way to bring this fairytale moment to life. The groom and guests get their first glimpse of the beautiful bride as she steps into the aisle. Often the bride is on the arm of a loved one such as her Dad. Frame this area with flowers to complete the perfect setting. By framing the end of the aisle with flowers, candlelight, garlands of greenery or a combination of those decorative elements, and asking them to pause there for effect you set the stage for the type of grand entrance many brides dream of.

If your budget allows you to invest in decorating the full aisle with floral materials, it will make quite a visual statement. However, this area should be secondary to the altar setting. The guests and photos will be focusing on the altar for a longer period of time so those decorations are most important. If you must cut costs by limiting the flowers used for the aisle, consider creating an entrance at the back of the aisle and decorating only the family pews of honor.

Measure the width of the aisle to be sure that placing décor on either side still leaves enough space for the wedding party to walk down the aisle in couples.

Ideas for creating an elegant entrance for the bride include:

• Mark rows of reserved seating for parents, grandparents, immediate family and honored guests with ribbons, tassels, bows, flowers, or greenery. Candlelight can be added to the decorations as well.

• Candlelight can be used in the aisle for evening weddings. The flames should be enclosed in glass or acolytes (faux candles) used. Check with your facility for rules and regulations on the use of candles. If candles are used, they can be lit in advance or as a part of the ceremony.

• A special aisle candle can be placed at the seat of the deceased parent or grandparent in their memory. You may choose to mention this detail in the wedding program.

• If creating a larger reserved seating area, place small 'between the ribbons' cards in the invitations of guests who are invited to sit in these pews of honor. The guest then presents their card to the usher who will escort them to this area.

• Shepherd's hooks can be used to create a tiered effect in the aisle. In advance, fill waterproof containers with plaster of paris; insert a Shepherd hook, or other tall holder, leaving a space at the top for later adding wet design foam. Let them sit to dry. Prior to the wedding, fill the top of the container with soaked foam and arrange flowers or greenery on top of the base container to create an arrangement. Add additional decoration by hanging flowers, floral orbs, bouquets, candles, etc. from the hooks. Be sure the base is weighted enough to keep the designs from overturning. Stones can be incorporated in the plaster of paris to make them heavier if needed.

• Use floral topiaries placed on the floor, as aisle décor.

• Create a window box effect with short rectangular containers placed on the floor beside the pews or chairs and flowers arranged in rows of varying heights and spilling over the edge to recreate the window box look.

• Have a group of small flower girls wearing floral halos (small garlands on their heads) enter before the bride, each carrying a fresh flower. They stand along each side of the aisle and as the bride passes them they hand her their flower. This collection of flowers she lays on the altar to signify the beginning of the ceremony.

• For an outdoor ceremony, use small draping green plant baskets such as ferns, ivies, etc. or blooming plants such as mums, geraniums, etc. and insert small candle torches or stands into the plants.

• At the shore, tiki torches adorned with flowers can be inserted into the sand to create an aisle. Or, a path can be marked by two rows of metal pails filled with sand to hold pillar candles in hurricane globes, surrounded by seashells. Paper luminaries can also be used to create a lighted pathway.

• Remember that not only is this aisle an entrance, but it is also an exit. If your budget allows, create your designs so that the back of the aisle also looks pretty to guests as they turn to watch you leave.

"A variety of seasonal soft-draping materials can be used to create garlands depending on your needs"

Hanging garlands

Fresh greenery can be hand-wired into lengths of garland or purchased from your local florist or supplier as pre-made garlands. A variety of seasonal soft-draping materials can be used to create garlands depending on your needs. Flowers, small fruits, cones and pods, or dried materials can be incorporated by wiring or gluing the items in place. A draping of fresh garland can add a lush decorative accent to highlight architectural details or embellish a plain area.

To measure for the use of garlands: measure the length of the area where it will hang. Use 1 ½ the length in measured footage to allow for draping. For example: to hang garland on a six foot rail, measure the rail to find the center and mark it by wrapping a wire around it in that spot. The wire should be covered in floral tape or coated in plastic to keep it from cutting into the finish of the rail. Cable ties, bind wire, chenille stems, heavy fishing cord, or thick string will also work for this purpose. Bend a nine foot length of garland in half to find the center. Attach that greenery center to the midpoint of your railing and use the wire from the rail to tie it securely in place. To add a decoration such as a bow or cluster of flowers, wire them in place as well. Attach each end of the greenery to either end of the rail by wiring it in place. Or, with permission of the facility you could place a small nail in each anchoring spot

Smilax Garland
Wired Garlands of Dendrobium Blooms
Cymbidium Orchids
Trailing Ivy
Wax Flower
Hydrangea
Roses
Stephanotis

"A draping of fresh garland can add a lush decorative accent to highlight architectural details or embellish a plain area"

Freesia
Chrysanthemums
Roses
Asiatic Lilies
Wax Flower
Seeded Eucalyptus Buds
Ivy Leaves
Smithers-Oasis® Copper Aluminum Wire

instead and wire the garland to the nail. Add any extra ornamentation by wiring it in place as well. This method of dividing the greens will insure that the garland drapes equally on either side.

To keep garlands fresh, mist them with water or a floral anti-transpirant and store in plastic bags in refrigeration until time for delivery. They should be kept optimally at temperatures of 34 - 36 degrees F. This will prevent freezing and will insure that they are not stressed by heat. Excessive hot or cold temperatures can cause fresh greenery to turn brown and shatter. If planning to hang garlands outdoors, then, be sure they will not be in freezing temperatures or direct sunlight. If the weather is warm and sunny, note the movement of the sun to be sure it won't move into position to burn the greens. If necessary, cover the garlands with paper, sheeting, or toweling to block the rays of the sun prior to the event.

Flower-Savvy Tip:

Mist rose petals with floral finishing spray or water and seal in a plastic bag in refrigeration to keep them fresh for use in decorating. Use them for sprinkling over cake layers, encircling candles with color, or scattered for texture on a tabletop.

A small food dehydrator can be used to dry flower heads and petals from the garden to create a floral potpourri. This pretty floral mix can be made from flowers in your garden or from the garden of a loved one. It may even be made by or used in honor of someone who is unable to attend. The potpourri can be tossed at the bride and groom by guests as the couple ceremoniously departs for their new lives together. It could also be placed in small decorative bowls on the tables, wrapped in netting for favors, or scattered about the tables as decoration.

Calla
Lily Grass
#9 Ribbon
Fitz Design Beaded Bracelet

"Consider designing a different bouquet for each bridesmaid to create greater visual interest"

Roses
Wax Flower
Strands of Pearls

Embellish the details

One way to individualize your wedding is to add elements that express your personal sentiments.

• Place roses at the altar for each of you to give to your new mother-in-law as a token of honor and commitment as you exit the ceremony

• Play special music in honor or memory of someone special and note the recognition in the wedding program. If the bride or groom is vocally talented they may choose to sing a song to their betrothed as a part of the service

• Light a unity candle of three candles - one for each family on the sides and a central one in the center to indicate the joining of families

• Burn candles in memory of a loved one who is deceased

• For your bouquet, select flowers used in your mother's wedding bouquet

• Have an honored guest read a favorite poem or passage on behalf of the couple

• Ask wedding guests to join in repeating a prayer or singing a favorite hymn

• Celebrate communion as a part of your wedding vows

• Include religious or cultural rites that are a part of each family's tradition

• Use your toss bouquet as your guest book table decoration then toss it to potential brides as you exit the reception

Edible décor

Entertain guests with edible décor that adds color and texture to your table. Spill nuts, dried fruits, pretzels, edible flowers or a combination of these snacks around the table centerpiece for guests to munch on while dancing. This is especially appreciated when alcoholic beverages are served. You may be surprised how quickly this thoughtful decoration disappears as guests enjoy snacking while they visit with friends and family.

Flower-Savvy Tip:
Add drops of water to a votive candle holder or spray the base of the candle with Pam® (cooking spray) to prevent the candle from sticking to the glass. Salt sprinkled in the bottom of the votive also works well.

Gerbera Daisies
Smithers-Oasis® 8 Inch Copper Wire Collar

"To capture the interest of your guests, use unique flowers or floral forms that are unexpected or have been placed in unusual settings."

Designing with flair

To capture the interest of your guests, use unique flowers or floral forms that are unexpected or have been placed in unusual settings. Consider placing a large arrangement on a low bench rather than a tabletop. Use a repetition of small vases of flowers instead of one larger one. A serpentine or S-shape of flowers is visually more interesting than a rectangular arrangement. A dramatic line of massed branches can incorporate more visual space into an arrangement while using a lesser number of flowers. Bold color combinations can often pique a viewer's interest as well. Look for adventurous ways to incorporate flowers to add visual flair to settings.

Flower-Savvy Tip:

Prepare a wedding first aid kit in advance. Include aspirin, smelling salts, antacid, breath mints, tissues, disposable wet wipes and a lint roller. Add in band-aids, clear fingernail polish, safety pins, a needle and thread, and sharp scissors. For a quick fix: a small mirror, nail file, hair spray, hair pins, feminine pads, tampons, extra panty hose, club soda, hydrogen peroxide, a Shout wet wipe or Tide pen. If there will be children outdoors add a small can of spray for insect bites and a bottle of water.

Curly Willow
Calla
Spray Roses
Roses
Gerbera Daisies
Asiatic Lilies
Kale
Smithers-Oasis® Wreath Form
Cut In Half & Placed Into a
Serpentine Shape

Calla
Aspidistra Leaves
Curly Willow Tips
Ribbon Binding

Reserved tables

If you are planning an informal reception of light foods such as hors d'oeuvres or desserts only, you may not feel the need to offer seating to all of your guests. However, consider offering a few reserved tables for elderly or handicapped guests. For some individuals, standing for long periods of time or balancing a plate of refreshments can be difficult. For their comfort provide a guest table for them and mark it 'reserved' with signage. If the guest is a close family member such as a grandparent, place the reserved table near the center of activity so they will still feel included in the festivities.

Tiger Tail Mokara Orchid
Roses
Silver Tussie Mussie

Cakes outdoors

Special consideration must be given when placing cakes outdoors. The cake needs to be shielded from direct sunlight, heat, wind and especially rain. The table that supports the cake must be placed on a firm foundation to prevent it from turning over. A plan for dealing with insects or house pets must be considered as well as an alternative plan for moving the cake indoors in case of inclement weather.

Cymbidium Orchids
Tiger Tail Mokara Orchids
Wax Flower
Celosia
Variegated Ivy

"Look to the season for your inspiration in natural materials that will enhance your designs."

Sunflowers
Bells of Ireland

Incorporate natural materials

Texture is the visual luxury of design, since tactile qualities can stimulate the sense of sight. Autumn is a great season to utilize the rich colors and textural emphasis of natural materials. Cones, pods, vines, sticks, fruits, stones, feathers, grasses, seashells, and other natural materials can add visual interest to an arrangement or bouquet. Look to the season for your inspiration in natural materials that will enhance your designs.

To incorporate materials in a design, dense items such as cones and pods can be glued in place. More flexible items like vines or bendable branches can be wired and inserted into foam or bound within a handle. Lightweight materials such as grasses, feathers or yarns can be woven into the structure of a design, or attached to its exterior. One end of a wood pick can be inserted into a piece of fruit and the other end inserted into

Rudbeckia
Curly Willow

wet foam to secure the item in an arrangement or bouquet holder. The wood pick will absorb water and swell, holding the item more firmly in place.

A collection of items such as massed cones, flowers, rose petals, fruits, seashells, mosses or stones can be spilled into a space to highlight an item. Natural materials can be used to encircle a cake stand, hurricane globe, or highlight a centerpiece of flowers. These elements can help to establish a theme, express a sentiment, or illustrate a season. If they could potentially damage a table or table cloth due to dripping, staining, or scratching – place a thin layer of plastic beneath the items and tuck in its edges so the protective covering won't show.

If fresh flowers are to be placed into a collection of items and you are concerned about their lack of a water source, add small water tubes to each individual stem and tuck the tubes out of sight.

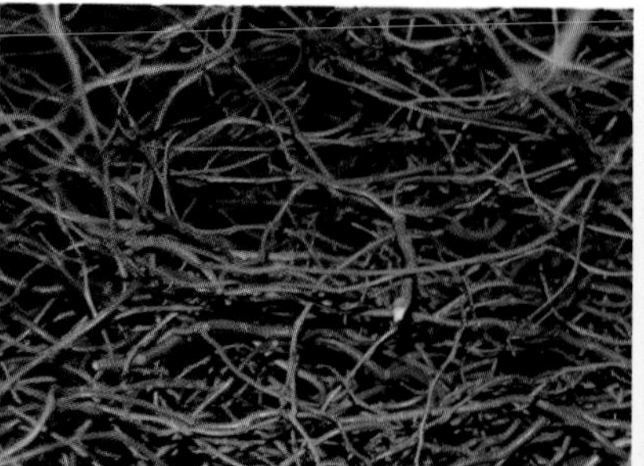

Sunflowers
Pine Cones
Fall Gourd

Planning at historical sites

Planning events at historical sites

Local sites of interest will often open their doors to hosted events as a means of additional income. Historical sites in your area might fall into this category.

Analyze your physical requirements

If you are considering a wedding at a historical site it is a good idea to visit the site and review the rules and regulations of the facility before making a final decision. In advance, formulate your plan of electrical, staging, water, kitchen space and lighting needs. Discuss those requirements with the site coordinator to be sure that the facility can accommodate those needs. Often older sites are not up to date technically, electronically, and with service provisions. Ask specifically if there will be enough parking, restroom, and loading/unloading areas to provide for your number of guests and size of event. Request a copy of their preferred vendor list or submit your selective list of professional service providers for their approval.

Check local regulations

Check with the facility coordinator or local authorities about local regulations regarding the serving of alcohol, noise ordinances or food service as applies to your event. Inform your vendors of the information that you receive. Ask them to sign off on any written materials, establishing that they have read, and agree to take responsibility for, following those directives.

Create itemized time schedules

In addition to the time required to host your wedding, check the facility schedule for availability of additional time for set-up and removal of food, performance, and décor displays as they apply to your event. Make a detailed schedule outlining the time needed on-site and get permission for these times in writing.

Develop a post-event 'to do' list

Many older sites have established guidelines that must be followed regarding the renter's responsibility for the post-event condition of the facility. Responsibility for cleanliness, position of furnishings, replacement of decor, etc. fall into this category. Establish who is responsible for these tasks (i.e. you or the facility). If action is required on your part, develop a plan for who will manage these tasks for you. Clarify any additional expense for this category.

Flower-Savvy Tip:

Be certain to appoint a responsible person to remain after the ceremony until all the photographs are finished in order to extinguish the candles. It is an easy task to overlook as everyone excitedly leaves for the reception. It is best to assign that important responsibility to a person who would be there anyway such as the spouse of an attendant or the parent of a child in the wedding party.

*"Ask for approval to publish images.
Secure permission in writing to release photographs, video, or other published images. Be aware of any restricted areas. Convey this information in writing to your vendors."*

Cymbidium Orchids
Callas
Hydrangea
Roses

Ask for approval to publish images

Secure permission in writing to release photographs, video, or other published images. Be aware of any restricted areas. Convey this information in writing to your vendors.

Request confirmation in writing

Once you work out the details of your event with the site coordinator, pay any required deposits, and then ask for a copy of the detailed agreement in writing. Since weddings are typically planned months in advance, it is possible that the employee that you made plans with no longer works there at the time of your event. This will prevent a new facilitator from having the opportunity to alter your plans or plan another event at the same time as yours.

Planning events at historical sites

- Analyze physical requirements
- Check local regulations
- Create time schedule
- Develop post event `to do' list
- Ask for approval to publish images
- Request confirmation in writing

Planificación de eventos en sitios históricos

- Analizar exigencia física
- Verificar las regulaciones
- Crear calendario
- Desarrollar una lista de cosas"para hacer" despues del evento
- Solicitar la aprobación para publicar imágenes
- Pedir la confirmación por escrito

By candlelight

Candlelight adds a soft, romantic glow to evening events. When mixing food and flowers, the elements of color and texture blend to create new and visually interesting color palettes. Flickering candlelight can play on these varied tactile surfaces to enhance the look. Varying the heights of candles from lighting the tabletop to lighting the atmosphere can create warm and inviting niche areas within a larger space.

Candlelight can be used to highlight areas or to direct the flow of guests from one area to another. Check with your facility for rules and regulations about using real candles. If allowing candles at all, many facilities require that they be kept in glass holders. If candles are not an option, faux candles called acolytes are available. Acolytes are shaped like candles and give off a similar amount of candlelight.

Flower-Savvy Tip:

Use candles to help create the ambiance you desire. To light the food, flowers and table coverings use candlelight 12 inches tall or less. To highlight the faces of your guests use candles that are 15—18 inches in height. To create a festive atmosphere use candles that are 24—36 inches tall.

Winter

A season of celebration and festive flowers

Holiday weddings

Planning wedding events during the holidays

'Tis the season to be jolly" ... that is unless you are a bride trying to plan an elegant event during a hectic time of year. There are many elements to consider such as a shortened length of time between seasons, extra expense, competing activities, existing facility décor and the possibility of inclement weather.

Limited Choice of dates and times

Select a date that will accommodate the availability of event locations, hectic seasonal activities of your family and friends, even your honeymoon travel plans. The holiday season is a shortened space of time during which many people compete for dates to book their social events. Often facilities book far in advance for these times so check out those availabilities first. Some church facilities have adopted the practice of refusing to book weddings during the holiday season to keep from conflicting with church activities. Consider all factors before selecting a date.

Allow for extra expense

If your chosen site does allow weddings in the Christmas season, ask about cost as sometimes there is an extra fee when a wedding will take place near the holidays.

While friends and family like to gather together for holiday celebrations, the extended list of family events, business, and social obligations that are scheduled in this short space of time can cause conflicts for both potential participants and guests. With guests

Roses
Spruce
Smithers-Oasis® Brown Aluminum Wire

already experiencing extra holiday expenditures as well, some brides have found themselves on the short list when it comes to wedding parties and gifts.

Travel to some locales can become more expensive and less available during the holidays so it is a good idea to check out the availability and expense of your favorite honeymoon preferences before setting a definite date. Also consider how the challenges of decreased time and increased money for travel might affect potential guests coming in from other areas.

Consider the weather

In some parts of the country, inclement weather is a factor to consider. Check the Farmer's Almanac in advance for a good guess on what weather might be expected. The almanac is quite accurate, relatively inexpensive, and can be ordered online at www.farmersalmanac.com.

If there is the chance of snowy or icy roads, consider having the ceremony and reception at the same site to diminish travel for the guests. For a small group, a hotel or bed and breakfast might be considered so that guests can stay overnight. Having the event earlier in the afternoon can keep guests off treacherous roads late at night. If driving could be difficult, you may also decide to forgo serving alcohol so that guests leaving your event can be more safely alert.

Use seasonal inspiration

If you plan to use traditional red and green colors, check in advance on your facilities decor and decorations for the season to be sure those bright colors will blend. You can adjust your color harmony to coordinate with their plans. Achieving a pleasing color palette that compliments is important visually to both guests and photography. If choosing a holiday theme, scatter beautiful ornaments on the tables as keepsakes for the guests. Use open weave decorative ornaments as the armature base for your bouquets as a memorable gift to your attendants. Decorate a Christmas tree with ornaments engraved with your guest's names on the front and their reception table seating number on the back. The tree will be an element of your decor and the ornament will guide them to their table and also be their wedding favor to take home.

Flower-Savvy Tip:

Be aware of exposing fresh flowers to freezing temperatures. When frozen, flowers turn brown and lose their form. In cold weather, cover flowers in plastic for delivery.

Nandina Berries
Smithers-Oasis® 6" Silver Wire Collar
Smithers-Oasis® Aluminum Wire
Smithers-Oasis® Silver Bouillon Wire with Pearls

While reds and greens are popular in this season, unless you want a holiday theme consider blending in some other rich hues. Jewel tones such as deep pink and purple, burgundy, royal blue, dull gold, and russet orange can be used to give a winter feel without a holiday motif. Evergreens, berries, cones, pods and branches can be used to enhance winter designs. Scatter faux jewels on the tables. Use glass mosaic votive holders to reflect the colors. Mix jewel-toned glass vases throughout the tables as containers for your flowers. Fill clear bowls with berries or cranberries and float candles in them.

For a winter wonderland effect, blend off white, ivory and blush tones mixed with soft metallics such a burnished gold, polished silver, or platinum to achieve a dreamy, romantic ambience. Faux iced branches, ice crystals and snow scattered over tables add to this pristine look. Cluster pots of tall, bare tree branches sprayed either gold or silver and lighted with tiny twinkling lights throughout the reception area. With the permission of the facility, pile deep drifts of snow (shredded white Styrofoam) around the bases of the trees to create an outdoor winter landscape effect. Place tall glass vases filled with faux snow (see resource guide) or imitation ice crystals holding long iced branches in clusters on tables. Bank with faux snow and tuck small votive candles at their base of vases for a soft, twinkling lights effect. Many facilities now require that you use battery operated lights. If you use electrically wired lights, be aware of the need to cover electrical wires running to outlets for safety reasons. An ice carving would fit perfectly with this icy winter look if it fits within your budget. Vases of flowers in blended whites interspersed throughout the room will complete this winter scene.

Create a sense of comfort

Appeal to the five senses to create a feeling of comfort and warmth on a cold winter's day or evening. Serve hot beverages such as hot chocolate, coffee, or hot tea upon the guests' arrival and offer 'to go' cups as they leave. Have musicians play holiday music as they enter the building. Spray the entrance with cinnamon fragrance or other holiday scent. If a fireplace is available have a roaring fire warmly greet your guests. Decorate with tabletops with textural materials such as evergreens, pods, and cones.

Provide a coat check area, a system for coats and wraps, and a person to oversee the process to eliminate confusion. If it is raining, offer a drive up area for the drop off of guests and men with umbrellas on hand to assist them. Strive to make guests as comfortable as possible.

Planning wedding events during the holidays

- Limited choices of dates and times
- Allow for extra expense
- Consider the weather
- Use seasonal inspiration
- Create a sense of comfort

Planificación de bodas durante dias festivos Dias a escojer limitados

- Gasto adicional
- Considere el tiempo
- Inspirar la decoracion de acuerdo a la epoca
- Crear un ambiente de comodidad

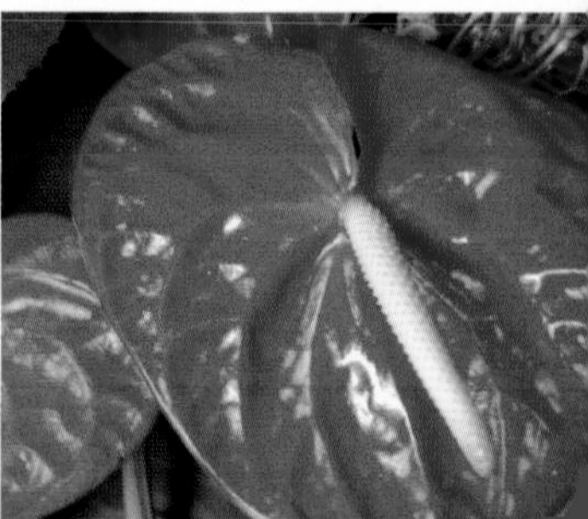

Roses
Nandina Berries
Smithers-Oasis® Silver Bouillon Wire with Pearls
Smithers-Oasis® Silver Aluminum Wire

Poinsettia trees

Working around church poinsettia trees
If a church allows you to schedule a wedding in their sanctuary during the holiday season, it is possible that you might have to work around their traditional holiday decorations. Be sure to add your signature look to existing items. Decorated Christmas trees, hanging wreaths and garlands, or poinsettia trees might have to be incorporated in your plan of decor. First, be sure the colors they plan to use match your chosen color harmony. Next, schedule a consultation with the decorator to find where the decorations will be placed. Then, develop your plan to include those items. Look for ways you can utilize their decorative elements, but add your accents and the placement of your wedding party in a way that makes the design style all your own. For example: this poinsettia tree has been framed by fresh arrangements of branches and berries on the baptismal rail before it, changing its look from traditional to 'trenditional'. Ask permission before removing or redecorating any items that the facility has put in place.

If planning a date near Easter you may face the same dilemma with an Easter lily or cross display. Check your calendar carefully for holidays when scheduling dates and be sure to ask the church contact about any special upcoming events near your wedding day.

Poinsettia Plants
Curly Willow
Nandina Berries
Nandina Foliage

Incorporating rich texture

When developing a setting for the presentation of food, flowers, or cakes look to the environment they will be placed in for inspiration. Incorporate the color and texture of both the surrounding area and other elements within the setting, into your master plan.

Flower-Savvy Tip:

When incorporating fruit into a flower arrangement, first insert a 4" or 6" wood pick into the base of the piece of fruit. Next place the fruit in its position in the design. Press the fruit to push the pick into the wet foam. The wood pick will absorb water from the foam and expand which will firmly hold it in place. Add fresh flowers and foliages around the fruit to complete the design.

Sliced pieces of fruit can be sprayed with fresh lemon juice or a floral finishing spray to keep the edges from turning brown.

The complex combination of fabrics, fibers, fruits, foods, and flowers mixed with wood, glass, and metal finishes creates the quintessential feel of the room. Tactile properties give substance to large displays. Even the backdrops, wall coverings, upholstery, and flooring of the room come into play in unifying a setting. The size, style and placement of furnishings matters, as well. It is ultimately more difficult to blend a wide variety of textural materials unless they express some commonality such as color, form, or feel. Seek to balance a varied group of elements by clustering them in groups for added impact and to create a more harmonious presentation.

Tiger Tail Mokara Orchids
Wax Flower
Celosia
Cymbidium Orchids

Roses
Nandina Berries
Spruce
Smithers-Oasis® Elegant Bouquet Holder

Using bouquet holders

For a finished look, it is important to cover the green or white plastic bouquet holders with a decorative treatment to hide the mechanics of the bouquet. Fresh foliages or floral materials can be glued securely onto the handles with cold adhesive or attached with double faced tape. Ribbon, fabric or other hard good materials can also be attached with double faced tape or glued in place with a hot glue gun. Flowing materials such as bear grass or strands of beads can be glued into holders that have hollow handles.

When decorating the handle of a foam based holder, it is best to do so while the foam is dry. Next, place the face of the foam in a shallow bowl to soak just the foam with water. Then, remove the holder and place it with the foam side down on a paper towel to drain before inserting flowers. This will prevent water damage to the decorative holder.

Using all white

When choosing an all white bridal bouquet, it is important to remember that fresh flowers reflect varied shades of white. Along with a crisp, clear white hue, there are also green, pink, and yellow shades of white. Consider the colors in your chosen palette that will be used in other designs and materials then select a shade of white that will harmonize. This will provide visual unity in your photographs.

A blend of whites works best against an all white dress, as it will make the bouquet advance visually for photography rather than blend into the dress. If choosing a candlelight (off white) dress, remember to incorporate ivory shades of white as well. For example, if choosing a blend of white roses to hold before a candlelight dress consider a collection of crisp white, champagne, and ivory tones. In floral design, green is considered a neutral and can be a perfect backdrop to whites.

Roses
Dendrobium Orchids
Nandina Berries
Foam Based Bouquet Holder

Accessorize with jewelry

The elegance of bride and bridesmaids' dresses is being matched by today's fashionable floral design. Jewelry too, isn't an accessory just to be worn by the girls anymore. Now bouquets and body flowers are equally adorned by jewel accents of their own. Pearls, beads, and metallic accents that once were reserved for dresses now complete the design of floral bouquets as well. This luxurious look says there is something very important to celebrate when even the flowers have dressed in their finest.

As the popularity of more revealing dress styles has grown, a body flower in the form of floral jewelry is often an accessory of choice. Whether flowers are fashioned into jewelry form or trendy pieces of costume jewelry are added to bouquets for visual interest, beads and baubles are primary to current design

Include a family heirloom

Sometimes a close family member might be unable to attend because of sickness or distance or we want to remember a special loved one who is deceased.

• A great way to honor them is to use a piece of their jewelry pinned to the ribbon of your bouquet handle or tucked into the appropriate mother's bouquet.

• A smaller pin-on brooch might be added to the flowers for the bridal headpiece.

• If a parent is deceased a small locket with their tiny photo can be pinned into the flowers and their memory travels down the aisle with the bride.

• A special piece of jewelry can also be added to the flowers of your most honored guests as a keepsake.

• Perhaps you want to give each mom a beautiful token of the day. If they wear charm bracelets, engrave a charm with your names and wedding date and pin it into the flowers.

• A small brooch can be the focal point of the corsage of flowers pinned on their dress.

• Search local flea markets for great finds in antique jewelry that can become the focal point of the mother's flowers.

• The same concept applies to interesting gifts for bridesmaids; a similar treasure can be tucked into their bouquet as a keepsake.

• Match a small evening bag to the dress of each mother, grandmother or other special guest and adorn with flowers. Give them on the day of the wedding as a memorable wedding gift.

• Glue flowers or jewels to round band-aids and stick them onto the skin as a floral tattoo.

Flower-Savvy Tip:

The combination of cold temperature and moisture requires that you select a cold-hardy floral adhesive, such as Oasis brand floral adhesive instead of hot glue when securing items that will be placed in refrigeration. For example, when placing small flowers into a garland, on the rim of a basket, etc. use Smithers-Oasis brand floral adhesive to glue them in place. Allow to completely dry before refrigerating. Small pieces of jewelery can be pinned in place.

Oriental Lilies
Hydrangea
Lily Grass
Ribbon
Vintage Broach

Oriental Lilies
Bear Grass
Linen Handkerchief
Vintage Broach

Oriental Lilies
Bear Grass Strung with Pearls
Ribbon
Vintage Broach

Dramatic floral cuffs

Create drama by wearing a floral cuff
The long, graceful lines of today's popular sheath, a-line, mermaid, and trumpet dresses create the perfect backdrop for the newest trend in wedding florals, vertical bouquets. Cascading from the wrist or even handheld, these elegant floral cuff bouquets are lightweight, easy to hold or wear, and add floral enhancement without hiding the beautiful bridal gown.

Armatures add visual interest
Tired of the look of massed bouquets, some brides are asking for structure once again with a little more formality and style than the 'loosely gathered from the garden' look. Armatures, hand-made mechanics or the look thereof, are increasing in popularity. They provide visual excitement as the flowers are intricately woven into the design. Often foliages are used as an intricate part of the bouquet design as are touches of feather, leather, and fur. Think of flowers tucked through the woven strands of a bird nest for a garden wedding, intricately woven metallic wire and beaded forms for a glitz and glam appeal, or natural vines weaved into a delicate form for an Eco-chic look. From luxe to luscious, these new design styles portray color and texture in an interesting form. Brides who hope to express their individual personality by the wedding flowers of their choice are often intrigued by these designs.

Flower-Savvy Tip:

Even when executing an all white wedding consider using off-white or ivory candles, ribbon, and paper products for a richer, more elegant look. Blended intensities of whites will afford more visual depth to this pristine color combination.

Curly Willow
Roses
Dendrobium Orchids
Eucalyptus Buds/Leaves/Plumosa Tips
Smithers-Oasis® Large Bravo Holder
Smithers-Oasis® Silver Metallic Wire
Smithers-Oasis® Silver Bouillon Wire

Flower-Savvy Tip:

Dusting stephanotis with baby powder or cornstarch then shaking it off can help to cover slightly bruised lines or brown spots.

If you don't a have floral preservative spray on hand, a mixture of one part white Elmer's glue and two parts water can be used to dip delicate flowers such as stephanotis or lily of the valley for extra longevity. Be sure to allow to completely dry before packaging for refrigeration.

If static cling is causing a problem with the skirts of bridesmaids dresses, pin small metal safety pins to the seams on each side to break the magnetic field and release the gathers and wrinkles.

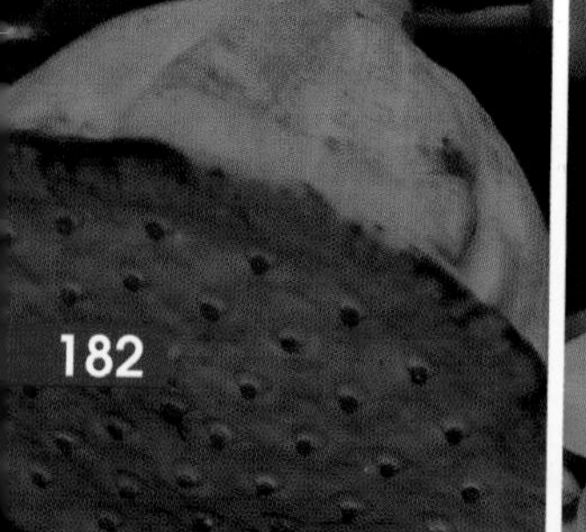

Phalaenopsis Orchids
Trailing English Ivy
Sprengeri – Clipped to Thin
Smithers-Oasis® 6 inch Gold Wire Collar
Smithers-Oasis® Gold Bouillon Wire
Smithers-Oasis® Gold Metallic Wire
Pearls Strung on Wire
4 Inch Gold Tassel

"An interesting new trend is for the bride to wear a small floral cuff or vertical bouquet for the reception"

Roses
Mini Callas
Hypericum
Smithers-Oasis® Silver Wire Collar
Smithers-Oasis® Silver Bouillon Wire with Pearls

Reception bouquet

An interesting new trend is for the bride to wear a small floral cuff or vertical bouquet for the reception. Often, a bride will choose a traditional bridal bouquet for her wedding ceremony and photos. While it is the perfect accessory for her formal gown and is the focal area of many of her photographs, it can be heavy or cumbersome to manage while dancing and mingling with guests at the reception. The reception bouquet is perfect for this purpose. Hanging delicately from the wrist, this lightweight design can be worn while dancing or greeting family and friends in the receiving line. It adds a touch of elegance to the bride's first formal dance with her groom and as she moves about her reception. Designed of flowers similar to the ceremony bouquet, this much smaller, uniquely formed version offers greater flexibility for all the reception activities.

Flower-Savvy Tip:

After designing corsages, boutonnières or hand-wired bouquets mist them with an anti-transpirant or finishing spray such as FloraMist by Floralife, place them in a plastic bag, and blow into the bag before sealing. The flowers will utilize the carbon dioxide and moisture to stay fresh longer. Place two pins per design in each package for pinning purposes. Refrigerate.

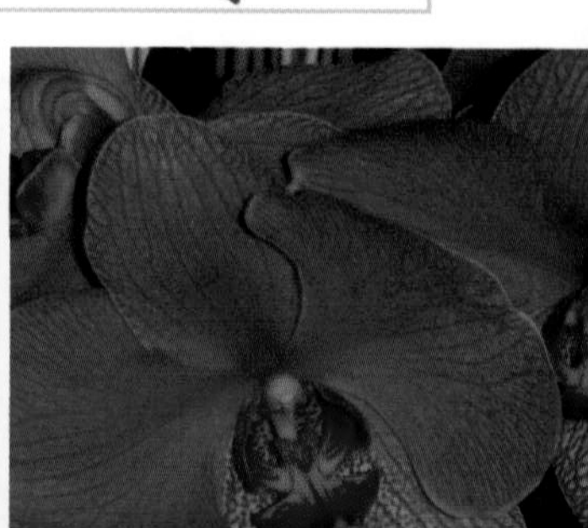

Cattleya Orchids
Sprengeri
Dendrobium Orchids
Dusty Miller
Wax Flower
Smithers-Oasis® Silver Bouillon Wire with Pearls

Cymbidium Orchids
Camellia Leaves
Smithers-Oasis® Elegant Bouquet Holder

Flowers and temperature

Flowers are living elements and can be harmed by excessive hot or cold temperatures. Prior to their use in design, they are best held in refrigerated temperatures of 34 – 36 degrees F. Tropical flowers are the exception, as they prefer warmer temperatures and should be kept at temperatures above 45 degrees F. Extra humidity can also be helpful for tropical blooms. Flowers and greens can lose their original shape, shatter, or turn brown if either sunburned or frozen. Proper care and handling is essential for flowers to remain fresh and beautiful.

If you are planning to deliver flowers to a wedding site through cold temperatures it is imperative that you wrap the flowers in paper or plastic to prevent the cold air from freezing them. It is a good idea to warm the delivery vehicle prior to placing the flowers inside. If flowers are to be displayed in snow, add a layer of plastic beneath them. Keep the flowers covered until just before guests arrive.

When displaying flowers outdoors in hot temperatures, direct sunlight can be a problem. Keep the flowers indoors until just before the event. Allow enough time for set up without leaving the flowers in the heat longer than necessary. Check the movement of the sun to be sure the flowers or greenery will not be in direct sunlight. If that is a problem, cover them lightly with paper or lightweight fabric until just before the event. Do not use plastic as the heat can build up beneath the plastic and speed the dehydration of the flowers. Provide optimal water levels for the flowers and mist them often with water or an anti-transpirant.

Phalaenopsis Orchids
Sprengeri
English Ivy
Lily Grass
Bear Grass with Pearls

Designing on a fur muff

A bride can achieve an elegant, vintage glamour look with a fur muff with flowers as her winter bouquet. The bouquet of flowers should be constructed like a large corsage - usually wired and taped. Accents can be added with cold adhesive glue. Once the design is constructed, spray with an anti-transpirant, cover with plastic, and refrigerate. Prior to wedding delivery, pin the bouquet in place on the muff with corsage pins. Feel the interior of the muff to be sure that the pins do not protrude through the lining.

The same techniques can be used with a faux fur muff or a fabric muff made of the same material as the bridal gown. Smaller versions can be designed for bridesmaids or junior bridesmaids, and petite ones for flower girls or mothers who choose not to wear a corsage.

Vintage muffs can often be found as bargains at flea markets, second-hand and antique stores. An assemblage of one-of-a-kind finds can form a unique collection. Each bridesmaid can carry an individually-styled muff creating an interesting and elegant look.

Abstract designs

Museums of Modern Art and ultra-contemporary hotels are popular wedding sites for some young bridal fashionistas. Consider abstract floral designs to continue the trend-savvy theme. Unusual form, eye-catching color, and interesting tactile materials can be incorporated into a bouquet for an exceptional look.

Flower-Savvy Tip:

Floral magnets may be a better choice for children than corsage or boutonniere pins when attaching flowers to their clothing.

Preserving your bouquet

Often brides wish to preserve their bridal bouquet as a memento of their wedding day. Preservation techniques vary by cost and degree of difficulty. The results often depend on the method and type of flowers used. Brides who dry their bouquets themselves often opt for the hanging upside down or drying in silica gel methods. Another choice is to have a professional freeze-dry the flowers for you. Investigate the options for preserving your bouquet in advance, decide on a process and gather the materials. If you will be leaving after the wedding for a honeymoon trip, ask someone else to initiate the process for you or give them instructions to deliver the bouquet to a professional that you have hired. Fresher flowers will result in a better preservation of your bouquet. If it will be a day or two before the preservation process can begin, mist the bouquet with water and seal it in a plastic bag in the refrigerator to keep it from prematurely drying out.

The most basic technique for preserving a bouquet is to hang the flowers upside down in a warm, dry, dark place. After several weeks undisturbed, check the flowers for degree of dryness. A lack of moisture will result in a papery look and feel. The length of drying time depends on the density of the blooms you are drying. When the flowers are dry to the touch and show no signs of mold or moisture, spray with several coats of spray lacquer or a cheap hairspray. The cheaper the hairspray the better as the level of lacquer will be higher. This method is inexpensive and easy to do, but the flowers will not hold much of their original shape or color and will have a limited shelf life.

Another method is to use silica gel to dry flowers. Silica gel is a drying medium that can be purchased from your local florist or craft store. Although more expensive than air drying, this method results in

Roses
Alstromeria
Mini Cabbage, Ornamental
Trailing Ivy, Wound Around Bouquet
Smithers-Oasis® Silver Bouillon Wire with Pearls
Foam Based Bouquet Holder
Ribbon Covered Handle
Ivory Tassels

"Keep flowers fresh - mist bouquet with water, seal in plastic, and refrigerate until preservation process begins"

flowers that keep their shape and color better and for a longer period of time. It is best to dry flowers individually in layers of silica gel in a closed container. This process can take from a few days to a couple of weeks depending on the density of the flower. Be careful not to leave the flowers in this drying medium too long or the flowers will become brittle. Follow the directions on the container of silica gel.

Silica gel can also be used to dry your flowers in the microwave using basically the same technique. Blooms dry best when placed in the gel individually and micro-waved one minute at a time. Allow flowers to cool thoroughly before removing from the gel. Remember that this product is toxic when ingested, so keep it out of the reach of children and pets.

The most realistic technique of preserving your bouquet is to have it professionally freeze-dried. This process takes about four weeks and is done by a technician who has the proper equipment. The flowers are frozen and their moisture removed in the vapor stage. It is the most expensive method, but provides the highest results in terms of quality, longevity, and depth of color. Locate a professional in advance who can freeze-dry your bouquet and make arrangements to have someone get your flowers to them as soon after the wedding as possible. The freshness of the flowers has a major impact on the quality of results.

Preserving your bouquet

- Preservation techniques and results vary
- Do-It-Yourself techniques
  - Hang to dry method
  - Layer in silica gel method
- Hire a professional
  - Preserved in silica gel
  - Freeze dried

La preservación del Bouquet

- Técnicas de preservación, los resultados pueden variar
- Tecnicas de Hágalo usted mismo
  - método de Cuelgar para secar
  - Capa de sílica
- Contrate a un profesional
  - preservacion en gel de sílica
  - Freeze dried

Flower-Savvy Tip:

Place blocks of floral foam atop a container of water containing floral food. Allow the floral foam to sink into the water on its own, not pressing it into the water, to prevent isolated dry spots in the center. Soak until the foam is totally submerged and heavy from its absorption of water. Most brands have small holes on one side to show you which side to place down into the water. The holes help water soak in faster.

When refrigerating flowers, be careful that the temperatures are kept warmer than 32 degrees. Most flowers prefer 34 – 40 degrees. Freezing will cause flowers to turn brown once they have thawed. Flowers will look water-soaked and transparent if they are frozen or freezing.

Oriental Lilies
Dendrobium Orchids
Sprengeri
Trailing Ivy

Decorating window sills

Decorating window sills

When decorating a facility it is important to concentrate on creating focal areas of interest first. In the initial plan, create a visual stage of decor in the primary area that guests will focus attention on. Next, if money remains available in the budget consider decorating highly visible areas on the periphery of the area. For example, in a traditional church setting once the decor of altar and aisle have been chosen one might consider decorating the window sills to complete the scene. If the windows are of an unusual shape or style or they are made of stunning stained or etched glass, they are an element that can be highlighted beautifully with fresh flowers or greenery and candlelight. Check with the rules of the facility to see what restrictions and reqirements there may be.

Flower-Savvy Tip:

Freezing taper candle in advance of their use will help them burn more slowly and drip less.

Place small sheets of clear plastic beneath open flame candelabra to catch dripping wax. Fresh greenery, green plants, flowers, or flower petals can be strategically placed to hide the plastic.

If candle wax has dripped on carpet or fabric, place a sheet of brown paper (such as from a brown paper bag) atop the stain. Use a warm iron above the paper to draw the melting wax into the paper. Be sure to test a very small area first. Never touch the warm iron directly to the carpet or fabric.

If candle wax has overflowed onto the church windowsill use a hair dyer to heat the wax enough that you can more easily remove it.

AND TEACH
NATIONS, BAPTIZING
SON AND HOLY GHOST

Offer guests something to toss as you depart

What first began as a simple ritual of tossing rice and grains over the departing couple as a means of wishing them a long life and fertility has evolved into an expanded list of options. Today's guests often send the couple away by tossing small items meant to express best wishes for good luck, romance, happiness, celebration or even as a token of fun. For example, small candies for a sweet life or faux snow to represent going out into the cold world together as one.

Suggestions for items to throw:

Rice, seeds, or grains
Birdseed
Sunflower seeds
Fresh flowers
Flower petals
Homemade potpourri
Fresh green or fall leaves
Preserved green or fall colored leaves
Dried herbs
Small fruits (raisins)
Small candies
Faux snow
Paper snowflakes
Confetti

Some couples provide guests with a little more action and offer:

Blowing bubbles
Lighting sparklers
Setting off fireworks

Consider selecting a toss material that reflects your personalities or wedding theme. Be sure to check with your venue for their rules and regulations. Many have restrictions on what materials may be used, if any at all.

Just married

Decorating the car

Car décor may be used to mark the arrival and departure of the bride and groom, or honored guests such as parents and grandparents. Often, the style or theme of the wedding flowers or personal style of the bride and groom will be incorporated into the vehicle décor as well.

Vehicle decorations can be as simple as a "Just Married" sign, or as elaborate as arrangements or garlands of greens and/or flowers attached to doors, bumpers, hoods, or front grills with suction cups on floral cages or wreath frames. Garlands can be wired with a covered (coated) wire. Great care must be taken with the mechanics of attaching floral items to prevent damage to the vehicle and to make sure they stay securely in place.

Many people hire a limo, vintage automobile, horse drawn carriage, or a trolley. Others prefer a more personal statement, using the couple's profession or hobby as their inspiration. When guests enjoy the surprise of watching the couple depart in an interesting way, festivities end on an upbeat note. In addition to traditional options, consider:

Horseback
Hot air balloon
Police car
Motorcycle with sidecar
Bicycle built for two
Race car
Helicopter
Fire truck

ACKNOWLEDGEMENTS

Primary photographer
Douglas McGukin
Cover and all studio photos
Douglas McGukin Inc.
407 McGukin Road
Bremen, GA 30110
770.301.1556
mail@douglasmcgukin.com

Contributing photographers
Jim Celuch pg. 46
Celuch Creative Imaging
810 Cookson Ave., SE
New Philadelphia, OH 44663
330.339.6777
www.celuch.com

Glenn Holmes
Carrollton, GA 30116

Jennifer Kemp Photography
pgs. 6, 7, 8, 10, 24, 52, 74, 184
720 Stonington Court
Gainesville, GA 30506
706.499.6485
jennifer@jenniferkempphotography

Allison Dudley
pgs. 12, 13, 14, 15, 31, 68, 80
www.allisondudley.com

Diane Douglass pg. 7
Diane Douglass Photography
www.DianeDouglass.com

Karen Goforth pgs. 201, 203
Irresistible Portraits by
Karen Goforth
1418 South Main Street
Kannapolis, NC 28081
704.933.5600
www.irresistibleportraits.com

Jim Maguire pgs. 54, 129, 186, 187, 200
James Maguire Photography
875 Moe Dr., Ste. B23
Akron, OH 44310
330.630.9050
www.maguirephoto.com

Tim McClain pgs. 64, 66, 122, 136, 144, 153, 154, 155, 156, 158, 159, 202
McClain Photography
126 Bankhead Highway
Carrollton, GA 30117
770.830.9595
www.mccphotos.com
www.mccphoto.smugmug.com

Eric McCarty
pgs. 3, 4, 5, 8, 11, 20, 26, 27, 96, 97
Photographic Observer
www.ericmccarty.com/blog

Ron Parks Photography pgs. 59, 64, 125, 127, 128, 130, 132, 134, 135, 137, 202
2321 San Antonio Street
Austin, TX 78705
512.476.8957
www.ronparksphotography.com

Rob Roux Photography pgs. 28, 29
828 Glasgow Dr.
Lilburn, GA 30047
770.696.4622
www.starlabproductions.com
rob@robrouxphotography.com

Ron White pgs. 22, 23
www.ronwhitephotography.com
251.316.3838

OASIS FLORAL PRODUCTS DIGITAL DATABASE
pgs. 46, 54, 129, 186, 187, 200
The images contained in the OASIS Floral Products digital database are the property of Smithers-Oasis and are subject to copyright protection. They may be used only in conjunction with the promotion of OASIS brand and LOMEY brand products. Use of any of the foregoing should be accompanied with the following statement: OASIS and LOMEY are registered trademarks of Smithers-Oasis Co. Used with permission.

Copy Editor
Cathleen Mack Martinez
Auburn, New York
315.253.2133
crmartinez@verizon.net

Proofing Editors
Debra Wahl
Villa Rica, GA 30180
Shoes928@yahoo.com

Jenny Scala
Alexandria, Virginia 22314

Graphic Artist
Dana Wedman
W Designs, LLC
www.wdesignsco.com

Spanish Interpretation
Miguel Angel Figueroa, AIFD
Floral Event Studio
San Juan, PR 00921
PUERTO RICO
787.473.0471
www.floraleventstudio.com

Thank you
Garden flower contributions:
Joyce Doss
Susan Garrett
Andrew McGukin
Jane Rigsby

Contributing brides:
Heather Lord Allen
Megan Perry De Luna
Dr. Gwyn Goodwin Navarro
Mandy Chapman Howard
Brandy Hobbs Maxwell
Leigh Evans Whitton
Lawren Thompson Hutchinson

'Pearl Sisters' assistance:
Michelle Perry White
Vonda LaFever
Susan Standerfer
Kim Morrill
Beth O'Reilly

Flower Girl and photo assistance:
Joan Cole
Susan Williams
Brenda Lord
Susan Brown
Nancy Dixon
Kelly Mace
Jacque Sir Louis

'Bunko' friends
Georgia Evans
Vicki Maxwell
Diane McLendon
Debra Wahl
Carole Walker
Melba Wilkins
Carol Williams

and to family and friends for their endless support and encouragement.

RESOURCE GUIDE

Cake Baker
Agnes Mitchell
770.258.5898
threergone@live.com

Floral Accessories
Fitz Design
www.creationsbyfitzdesign.com
800.500.2120

Floral foam, floral wire products
Smithers-Oasis®
www.smithersoasis.com/us/floral

Orchids
Amy's Orchids
www.amysorchids.com
sales@amysorchids.com

Ribbon
Lion Ribbon and Berwick Offray
800.551.5466

Snow Real
JRM Chemical
4881 Neo Parkway
Cleveland, OH 44128-3101
Attn: Dave Czehut

Styrofoam
STRYOFOAM™ Brand Foam
from the Dow Chemical Company
www.stryofoamfloral.com

Dressmaker's form
Mears Floral Products
1222 S Scenic
Springfield, Mo 65802
800.533.7043

Fresh Garlands
Wm. F. Puckett, Inc.
PO Box 298
Barberville, FL 32105-0298
800.426.3376

AIFD
American Institute of Floral Designers
720 Light Street
Baltimore, MD 21230
www.aifd.org

With nearly 1,400 members worldwide, AIFD and its members are in the forefront of the industry in presenting educational and design programs. Accredited members of the American Institute of Floral Designers are distinguished by the letters "AIFD" used as addenda to their name.

AAF
American Academy of Floriculture
Society of American Florists
1601 Duke Street
Alexandria, VA 22314
www.safnow.org

Members of the American Academy of Floriculture share an honor that can be achieved by those individuals meeting the Academy's high standards of service to their industry and community. Nomination and acceptance into the Academy is open to qualified persons in all segments of the industry.

PFCI
Professional Floral Communicators – International
Society of American Florists
1601 Duke Street
Alexandria, VA 22314
www.safnow.org

PFCI is the floral industry's speakers bureau, a network of professional floral business educators certified by the Society of American Florists.

INDEX